Diffe   rains

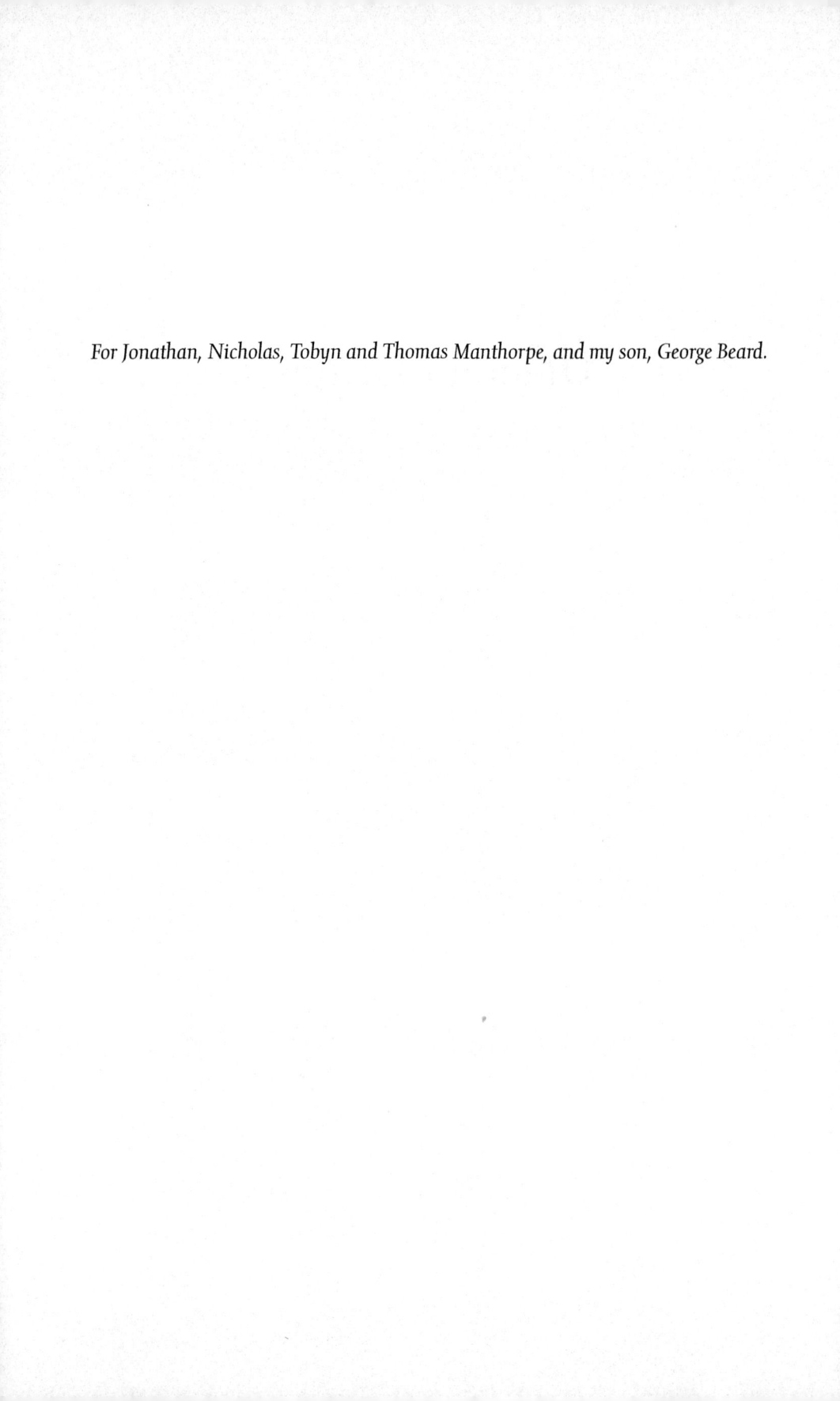

For Jonathan, Nicholas, Tobyn and Thomas Manthorpe, and my son, George Beard.

Different Drums
One Family, Two Wars

Victoria Manthorpe

Poppyland Publishing

Copyright © Victoria Manthorpe.
This edition 2024 published by Poppyland Publishing, Lowestoft, NR32 3BB.

www.poppyland.co.uk

ISBN 978 1 869831 34 9

All rights reserved. No part of this publication may be reproduced, stored in a retrieval system or transmitted by any means, mechanical, photocopying, recording or otherwise, without the written permission of the publishers.

Designed and typeset in 10.5 on 13.5 pt Gilgamesh Pro.

Printed by TL Books, Padstow.

Picture credits—see List of Illustrations p.7.

Front cover: *No More War demonstration on the Haymarket, Norwich, 1920s or early 1930s. Source unknown.*
Back cover: *photograph of author by Alan Lyall.*

Contents

List of Illustrations	7
Acknowledgements	12
Introduction	13
1. 1914–1916	17
2. 1916–February 1917	35
3. Spring 1917	49
4. Spring/Summer 1917–Autumn 1917	61
5. September 1917–February 1918	75
6. New Year 1918–1920	87
7. 1920–1937	101
8. January 1938—February 1939	117
9. March 1939—New Year 1940	131
10. January 1940—July 1940	141
11. Summer 1940—February 1941	153
12. February 1941—May 1942	163
Afterword	173
Appendix 1	175
Appendix 2	181
Appendix 3	183
Appendix 4	184
Appendix 5	185
Appendix 6	186
Appendix 7	189
Bibliography	191
Index	195

Also by
Victoria Manthorpe

The Japan Diaries of Richard Gordon Smith

Children of the Empire: The Victorian Haggards

Lilias Rider Haggard: Countrywoman

List of Illustrations

Unless otherwise credited, the photographs are in the possession of the author's family.

1: 1914–1916

1. The corner of St Stephen's Street and Surrey Street, Norwich circa 1910. *Postcard circa 1910.*
2. Model anvil and hammer that were Hamilton's apprentice pieces. *Kind permission of Jonathan Manthorpe.*
3. Hamilton and Eliza Manthorpe.
4. Avenue Road School class from 1897 with teachers Miss Tennant (far left) and Mr Smith (far right). Walter is in the top row, last boy on the left.
5. First-Day Adult Schools notice of meetings November 1890.
6. Hamilton's Peace Pledge 1893.
7. Members of the Society of Friends outside Goat Lane Meeting House, Norwich. Hamilton Manthorpe, seated on ground with legs out, front row second from left.
8. Hamilton (standing top left) with his two daughters (seated on step), Matilda and Anne outside Goat Lane Meeting House.
9. Hamilton' Coffee stall outside St Andrew's Hall.
10. The staff of Eddington's grocery shop on Gentleman's Walk. Walter is 5th from the right.
11. Boys' Life Brigade 1910. Norwich, location unknown.
12. A mixed hockey team at Westfield, Eaton Village. Walter middle row, centre left.
13. Eliza Manthorpe outside 51 Connaught Road, Norwich.
14. Walter (left) with Arthur Breeze camping at Whitlingham, on the outskirts of Norwich.
15. Walter Manthorpe outside his shop in White Lion Street, Norwich 1914.
16. Jane Swann.

2: 1916–February 1917

17. Matilda Jermy née Manthorpe, who actively supported her brother's pacifism.

18. Interior of Norwich Prison Hall. *Postcard.*

3: Spring 1917

19. Wormwood Scrubs circa 1917. *Postcard.*

20. A comic postcard from Wormwood Scrubs.

4: Spring/Summer 1917–Autumn 1917

21. Entrance to Dartmoor Prison. *Postcard.*

22. Coal party at Dartmoor.

23. Contemporary view of the village of Princeton and the Work Camp.

24. The COs Landing Stage at Loch Leven. The nearest village was 4 miles away. Walter was here from April to June 1917.

25. The wooden huts which formed the work camp at Caolasnacon.

26. Group of COs at Caolasnacon Camp, in front of a hut labelled 'The Jawbox' by Walter, who wrote the sign, is standing back row, fourth from right.

27. Walter kept this photograph folded in his wallet and it looks to be of a group of COs in a landscape of ferns and rocks that could well be the climbing expedition to Ben Nevis.

28. Wakefield Prison cells.

29. Cell at Wakefield Prison.

30. Exercise rings at Wakefield Prison.

5: September 1917–February 1918

31. Entrance archway to Dartmoor Prison.

32. Punishment cells at Dartmoor.

33. Interior of punishment cell.

34. Interior of the chapel at Dartmoor.

35. Inscription on reverse: Some artists at Dartmoor 1917. Second man from left was a tenor in Carl Rose Opera Co, a painter also." The names on the reverse are: far right Wiggins, front Willington and Smith, back row, Davies, Goulding, Shipp, Goulding, Cooley.

LIST OF ILLUSTRATIONS

6: New Year 1918–1920

36. William Henry Firth from the Peace Pledge union website The Men who Said No. *https://www.menwhosaidno.org/men/men_files/f/firth_henry.html*—With permission of the Peace Pledge Union, accessed 25/07/23.

37. Frederick William Swann in the uniform of the Royal Flying Corps in which he served as a clerk. *Courtesy of Brian Swann.*

38. A group picture of the COs from Norwich at Princeton, Dartmoor 1917/18. Walter top left. Most probably taken at the time of Mr Frith's funeral.

39. Carrying Mr Frith's coffin. It was a misty day.

40. Hall 7 Football team at Dartmoor. Names unknown.

7: 1920–1937

41. Past president Norwich District Grocers' Association badge.

42. Walter and Jennie in the 1920s.

43. Walter and Jennie in their back garden 1926.

44. The League of Nations Union ballot paper. *Courtesy of Judith Merrill and reproduced by Robert Bilbie.*

45. Young Walter aged about 19. Photographed at Coe's.

46. Taking the CSI exams in London 1930s.

47. Sketch of young Walter with glasses.

48. Walter's sketch of the newly built Shakespeare Memorial Theatre at Stratford-upon-Avon dated 1936.

49. Walter beside the Seine with the exhibition and the Soviet pavilion in the background, 1937.

50. Walter in front of the Place de Varsovie, Paris 1937.

8: January 1938—February 1939

51. Programme of a pageant called The Light of Youth. *Kind permission of Francis Banfield.*

52. Youth House exterior, 250 Camden Road, London. *Kind permission of Gillian Etherington and Christine Betts.*

53. The common room at Youth House. *Kind permission of Gillian Etherington and Christine Betts.*

54. Dining room of Youth House. Date: Christmas early or mid-1930s. Two women sitting centre of picture are Winifred Shields and Maud (?). The man sitting front right is Nunc Reilly, one of the Theosophist founders. Interior of Youth House. Date: possibly Christmas 1932. *Kind permission of Kevin Tingay.*

55. Youth House magazines and a pamphlet from The World Youth Peace Conference of 1928. *Kind permission of Gillian Etherington and Christine Betts.*

56. Marjorie Hutchinson, Louie Grimm and Jane (?) working in the kitchen at Youth House. *Kind permission of Gillian Etherington and Christine Betts.*

57. Members in the garden of Youth House. Exact date unknown. *Kind permission of Valerie Collinge.*

58. Young Walter's Peace Pledge.

59. The cottages called White Houses, Tring. *Kind permission of Gillian Etherington and Christine Betts.*

9: March 1939—New Year 1940

60. Women members in the garden at Youth House. *Kind permission of Kevin Tingay.*

61. Walter's Peace Pledge Union lapel badge. *Kind permission of Jonathan Manthorpe.*

62. Anne Parker and Walter Manthorpe in Germany July 1939.

63. Brasserie Universalle, Piccadilly Circus. *Postcard.*

10: January 1940—July 1940

64. Jack Manthorpe aged about 18.

65. Jack with some of his friends third from right, Peggy Cann to his right and Mel Cann, second from left.

66. The Shire Hall, Lancaster Castle.

11: Summer 1940—February 1941

67. Group picture taken after the Swingler-Shields wedding at Youth House August 1941. *From a copy in the possession of Valerie Collinge. Location of the original picture unknown.*

68. Jack at Horning, Norfolk aged about 19.

69. Jack age 21 in his RAF uniform.

12: February 1941—May 1942

70. Interior of St Margaret's Church, King's Lynn.

71. The Wincarnis Factory, Westwick Street, up in flames. *permission of NCC Picture Norfolk.*

Afterword

72. Walter Manthorpe senior in his health food shop in the 1960s. *(photographer unknown)*

Acknowledgements

There is no question that this book would never have been written without the encouragement of the late Anthony Thwaite who liked the sound of the subject and thought it worth writing. After his death, his wife Ann continued to take an active interest, for which I am most grateful.

Many people helped with research by responding quickly and generously to my enquiries: Francis Banfield, Christine Betts, Valerie Collinge, Val Deagley, James Eddington, Gillian Etherington, Prof. Richard Jackman, Prof. Peter Liddle, Jonathan Manthorpe, Judith Merrill, Prof. Ann Oakley, W. Martin Shepherd, Sylvia Stevens of the Goat Lane Meeting, Brian Swann, Kevin Tingay and Martin Val Baker.

I am most grateful to people who took the time to read some early ideas and proposals: Penny Clarke, Prof. Richard Jackman, Prof. Philip Mosley, and Evelyn Toynton. Thanks also to Paddy Hartnett for preliminary editing help.

We are very blessed in this country with willing and enthusiastic library staff, archivists and volunteer archivists who maintain our historical records. I am indebted to the people who helped me at the following institutions:

> Blackpool History Centre Library
> Bradford Local Studies Library
> Imperial War Museum
> The Maddermarket Theatre
> The Norfolk and Norwich Millennium Library
> The Norfolk Record Office
> The Peace Museum, Bradford
> The Peace Pledge Union Archive
> RAF Disclosures, RAF Cranwell
> The Society of Friends
> The Vegetarian Society Archive.

Lastly, I am very much obliged to Gareth and Janet Davies for undertaking publication, and all the work that goes with it.

Introduction

If a man does not keep pace with his companions, perhaps it is because he hears a different drummer. Let him step to the music which he hears, however measured or far away.

Henry David Thoreau—Walden, 1854.

After my mother died at nearly 100 years of age in 2014, I came into possession of boxes of family letters, papers and photographs. It was some years before I started sorting through them with a view to reducing their number. I knew there was quite a lot of material relating to my grandfather, Walter Manthorpe, and his time as a conscientious objector during World War I and so, with family members now living in different countries, I thought it would be worth compiling an account for future generations. When I discovered that there were also letters, appointment diaries, and memorabilia from the 1930s and early 1940s that related to my father's pacifism in World War II, as well to his brother, Jack, an RAF pilot, I could see there was the possibility of telling a larger story. I began reading around the history of the subject, as well as memoirs and literature of the period, and also contacted some descendants of my parents' contemporaries. From historian Martin Ceadel's wide-reaching study, *Pacifism in Britain 1914-1945: The Defining of a Faith*, I could see that our provincial family history perfectly illustrated the national development of pacifism from a Liberal and non-conformist political culture in 1914 into a somewhat uncomfortable humanitarian and internationalist response to Nazism in 1939.[1] I also saw that our papers included material that wasn't covered elsewhere, particularly about an organisation called Youth House, and the intergenerational discussion of pacifism. So, the proposed account became a longer project and this is the result.

This is a Norwich story and I have tried to name all the other Norwich COs that my grandfather came into contact with because they all supported each other and identified strongly with Norwich. Where I could I have added their details in the Endnotes, but some I have been unable to trace.

My grandfather, Walter Manthorpe, was not a political radical. He was a quiet Quaker from a working-class background. The family had migrated relatively recently from the fishing port of Yarmouth to the city of Norwich which, in those days, had the character of a large market town in an essentially agricultural county. Quakers, while extreme or literal in their Christianity, were well-integrated into society and they were not usually evangelical. When I knew him in the 1960s and early 1970s my grandfather's social views were old-fashioned and his personal style was conservative. He was a short, spry man with white hair, and despite a deeply lined face, a generally healthy appearance. He dressed well but not flamboyantly—he was recognisable by his homburg hat, his small cigars, his neat good-quality suits and waistcoats. Like many Quakers, he lacked a sense of humour but in his youth he had cultivated ambitions beyond his working-class background and he achieved them by becoming a pioneer of healthy diet and the proprietor of a health food store long before they were commonplace. He described his politics as Liberal and his radicalism, such as it was, focussed on the sacredness of human and animal life and on the limits of the authority of the state.

By refusing to comply with conscription for military service, he knew that he was doing something out of the ordinary. He was thirty-one years old when his time came and the consequences and experience of becoming a conscientious objector created his personal authority and marked the culture of our family. But, of course, in the wider scheme of things he was one of many—probably around sixteen thousand in a country of thirty-six million people—and his story was not more significant than others. He did not lead a revolt or write an inspiring tract or book. He was not one of the 'absolutists' who wouldn't make any concession. He suffered a good deal of ill-treatment that nudges well into the category of torture, but not as much as some. But after the war he did remain quite steadfast in his views and supported the No More War Movement in the 1920s and 1930s.

His sons called him The Guv'nor. It was a common enough form of address to fathers in the 19th century—the Governor—the pilot, the captain. But a governor is also a piece of industrial machinery for regulating the passage of gas, water or steam to ensure a regular motion. It's a self-acting contrivance. And in that sense, too, Walter was the 'governor' in our family, the moral regulator. But in a national context Walter was more like one very small but not insignificant pebble because as one commentator concluded, "The peace movement was the grit in the machinery; and perhaps all machinery ought to have some grit in it, even if only to ensure its regular inspection."[2]

Walter's surviving letters, mostly to his Quaker sister Matilda, from the prisons and camps to which he was sent were subject to censorship and therefore much was left unsaid. In 1974 he was interviewed by the Imperial War Museum about his experiences so there are tapes of his reminiscences in old age. These are informative but distinctly mellow; he easily makes excuses for how he was treated and he omits some of the worst experiences. Time had glossed over if not healed the events. In addition, there were newspaper interviews over the years and fragments of recall in letters and one typed statement. Throughout his life he stood firmly by his moral position: that did not change. He took a long view. And he was steady, completely steady.

My father was another matter. Physically much larger than his father, he was clever, artistic and imaginative. He pursued intellectual interests. He was not only *not* a Quaker, he was an atheist. He grew up in the 1930s which Auden so memorably called 'a low dishonest decade' and also, perhaps more relevantly to this story, an age of anxiety. What seems to occur is not a natural transition from non-conformity to humanitarianism but a lurching and shuddering into a new situation. Certainly, my grandfather found it difficult to follow my father's godless reasoning with regard to pacifism. In the twenty years between the wars a chasm had opened up.

My father was articled to a firm of Norwich surveyors and to gain his qualifications he had to go up to London quite often to prepare for and take his exams. He stayed at a singular institution in Camden Town called Youth House which, when he moved up to London to work, became the focus for his domestic, social and intellectual life. Youth House was a vegetarian hostel, unusually at the time catering for both men and women. It had been founded in 1927 by a group of Quakers and Theosophists bringing together two mystical belief systems. Quakerism had originated as a 17th century Christian sect that believed all humans had the capacity for a direct knowledge of God. Theosophy was a 19th century occult movement with roots in Gnosticism and Eastern esoteric practices. Theosophists were devoted to promoting the universal brotherhood of humanity and the essential oneness of creation. The objects of Youth House were... "to provide an experiment in communal living based on the ideal of service, a meeting place for young people of all nations, and an opportunity for Youth to gain self-expression along its own lines." Members organised a wide variety of recreational and educational activities as well as working for the Peace Council and the British Youth Peace Assembly. Soon it extended membership to non-residents; the woman who was to become my mother, Anne Parker, was one of the non-resident members. In a 1937 leaflet, the pioneering social researcher Richard Titmuss, who was one of the organisers, wrote: "The purpose of Youth House, therefore, is to produce rebels who would willingly conform to what little is sane in society to-day but who would rebel against all that is cruel, unjust, stupid and tyrannous."[3] Titmuss became the founding chair of social administration at the LSE and one of the architects of the Welfare State.

When World War II broke out Walter was only twenty-three and, through Youth House activities, had already aligned himself with pacifism. It was, as we know from hindsight, a very different war from the previous one, although it took some time for people to recognise it. When they did understand the implications of Nazism, many well-known people rapidly abandoned their anti-war stance—notably Bertrand Russell, A.A. Milne, C.M. Joad, Rose Macauley and Fenner Brockway. Inevitably, the notion of individual dissent has always been part of our family culture. Yet I cannot recall anyone in the family ever raising questions about the psychological roots of why people dissent—or, for that matter any psychological effects. It has been noted by several authors that it took a particularly bloody-minded kind of individual to stand up to the prevailing national opinion and one who valued 'the supremacy of conscience over the right of majority government.'[4]

It could be argued that they were deliberately forging an alternative mode of political dissent.[5] On the other hand, some people thought it was an avoidance of responsibility or that it was 'only too often the fruit of an unadmitted neurosis,'—a public response to private psychological distress.[6] The World War II COs were often artistic, broadly middle class, professionals or office workers, humanitarian rather than religious, and often wanting sexual freedom. Martin Ceadel's summing up of their position was: "Taken as a whole the younger generation of thirties pacifists represented within the British tradition of dissent a transitional stage between the nonconformist conscience and the beatniks."[7] I cannot imagine that my father would have recognised himself in that description, but he was certainly not conventional.

In World War II, to avoid repeating the persecution of the Great War and making martyrs, COs were rarely imprisoned but instead were allowed to fall into a void with regard to society; the state made sure it was nigh on impossible for them to work. There was no fellowship of conscience and no succour from religion. They were socially ostracised and economically isolated. My father's experience was, therefore, entirely different to his father's and played out in different ways. Nevertheless, the last thing he spoke to me about before he died was his deep awareness that he had been spared the fate of so many of the young men of his generation. It was no wonder that this haunted him: his younger brother, Jack, joined the RAF and died in 1942. From him, too, there are surviving letters.

Martin Ceadel called the real achievement of Britain's early-20th century peace movement the ongoing intellectual conversation it created about war and its causes.[8] I would add that the very fact of conscientious objection being a recognised and legitimate strand of our national history has established the foundations for subsequent peace movements in the West such as the Campaign for Nuclear Disarmament, the War Resisters League and the Committee for Non-Violent Action against the Vietnam war, and the Not-In-My-Name protest against the war in Iraq. The grit is still in the machine.

Notes

1. Ceadel, Martin, *Pacifism in Britain 1914-1945: The Defining of a Faith*, 1980, p. 24.
2. T.G. Otte in a *Times Literary Supplement* article quoted in https://www.encyclopedia.com/arts/educational-magazines/ceadel-martin-eric-1948, accessed 31/1/23.
3. Youth House publication, *Youth House: Past Present Future*, 1937.
4. Ceadel, pp. 268 and 303.
5. Ibid., p. 228.
6. Leslie Paul. *Angry Young Man*, 1952, pp. 284 and 238. Leslie Paul started out as pacifist and changed his mind. This seems to be the first use of the term 'angry young man' which resurfaced as a popular term in 1956.
7. Ceadel, p. 232.
8. *Times Literary Supplement* article quoted in https://www.encyclopedia.com/arts/educational-magazines/ceadel-martin-eric-1948, accessed 31/1/23.

1. 1914–1916

To most English people in the high summer of 1914 the prospect of a European war was almost unimaginable. The bonds of trade, culture and governing royalty were extensive and had been strengthened by King Edward VII's diplomacy. No one had foreseen that the assassinations of Archduke Franz Ferdinand of Austria and his wife at Sarajevo on June 28th would ignite two sets of political alliances into hostile opposition. By a series of treaties Germany, Austria and Italy were lined up against Russia, France and England. Long-standing rivalries and a complexity of national ambitions burst into action: Germany seized the opportunity to declare war on France on August 3 and invaded neutral Belgium.

The British Liberal and left-wing press were, at first, against any involvement as were the Liberal provincial papers; the feeling was that England was only marginally implicated in the quarrel.[1] Beyond a tolerance of the status quo and a distaste for involvement, there was also the fact that the country was ill-prepared for a fight on land. Great Britain relied for defence on her strong navy; her professional army, which was deployed all over the Empire, did not exceed 120,000 men. When Britain declared war on Germany on 4 August, several members of Prime Minister Asquith's Cabinet resigned and Lord Kitchener, the Secretary of State for War, had a job on his hands to prepare the armed forces.

Initially, idealism was high and early campaigns to encourage enlistment were successful. Kitchener's aim was to raise 100,000 men. The upper classes, already invested in Imperial and regimental culture, responded almost as a matter of course. Amongst the middle and working classes, whole offices, workshops, football teams and estate labourers joined up together as 'Pals'. These were groups of colleagues in the same regiment which ensured that regional, class and religious rivalries were not a source of disruption. There were joining fees for some regiments in order to ensure social exclusivity. Many firms guaranteed the jobs of their workforce upon return, as people saw the war as a short, sharp endeavour to teach the militaristic Germans a lesson.[2] On the other hand, high unemployment levels meant that many of the poorest and the dispossessed seized the opportunity for any regular employment, especially with food and clothes provided.

In Norwich in early August there was a Labour protest against the war with a demonstration in the Market Place by the International Socialist Bureau who passed a resolution against the Alliance.[3] But by the end of the month there was a public meeting at St Andrew's Hall to recruit volunteers and within a week 2,500 had enlisted.[4] According to the *Eastern Daily Press* of 14 August, just ten days into the campaign, national recruitment was at 8,000 a day and during the first four months of the war, a million men joined up. These recruitment meetings were staged in much the same way as religious meetings and often with religious speakers which gave them a moral validation.[5] Very soon German residents in England had to register their identities although in Norwich, unlike other parts of the country, there was no violence or overt ill-feeling expressed toward them.[6]

From its position facing the Low Countries, Norfolk was on the front line for attack with Weybourne and Happisburgh thought to be particularly vulnerable to invasion. The herring fleet was ordered back to port and all fishing suspended. Boy Scouts were deployed to keep surveillance along the coast. The fears were justified. In November 1914 Yarmouth and Gorleston were bombarded by artillery from a German ship off shore. There was no question that the country was at risk. In January 1915 Yarmouth and Lynn were bombed by Zeppelins. Local Emergency Committees were set up; there were strict blackouts to protect Norwich from casual bombing and preparations made to receive refugees from Belgium.

The 1st battalion of the Norfolk Regiment saw action at Mons in August 1914 where casualties reached 1,600. By the end of the year half a million British soldiers had been wounded or missing in action. Already there simply weren't enough soldiers to throw into the maw of warfare. There was mounting pressure to recruit volunteers and public antagonism and racial hatred towards Germany was goaded by the Shelling of Rheims Oct 1914, the Bombardment of Hartlepool and Scarborough in December 1914, the Zeppelin raids (on Yarmouth, Sheringham and King's Lynn, February, 1915), and most especially by the sinking of the Lusitania in May 1915. However, this didn't necessarily translate into volunteers.

In August of 1915, the 17th Earl of Derby, Lord Kitchener's Director General of Recruiting[7] devised a voluntary Recruitment Plan. He had misjudged the public mood. Men were no longer rushing to show how brave or patriotic they were. The high casualties and the growing knowledge about the dreadful reality of trench combat were already a big deterrent. The public might support the war but enthusiasm for voluntary enlistment had subsided.[8]

In January 1916 the government introduced conscription under The British Military Service Act which provided that all single able-bodied men between 18-41, and childless widowers, were deemed to have *already* 'enlisted' and were in Reserve battalions. This was later extended to married men, and later still to men up to 51 years of age.[9] Most significantly for this story, and most surprisingly in some ways, the Act not only clarified some occupations that were to be exempted or reserved and special circumstances but also that exemptions would be available to "conscientious objectors". Conscription was an innovation, but so was the possibility of exemption. This was extraordinary, and singular to Britain amongst all the warring nations.[10]

Conscientious Objectors was a designated category of men who had a moral or spiritual objection to war. A young friend of Lytton Strachey is supposed to have said in his own defence, "Madam, I am the civilization you are fighting for."[11] This may be apocryphal and is certainly facetious, but the statement has some validity since it was felt by many in Britain that the aspirations of Western European civilization were at stake. The Act came into effect in March of 1916 and a Non-Combatant Corps was created that allowed for those with partial exemption to serve as stretcher bearers and hospital porters. Resisters would be examined in civil courts. This was the national position in the early months of World War I. The problem was not in the Act itself but in its subsequent administration.

Norwich was generally a peaceful county town with a long history of non-conformity—Methodism, Unitarianism, Congregationalism—with Quakerism being particularly strong. It also had a tradition of regional provincial culture in painting, music, literature, applied design, and in printing. An early 19th century strain of political radicalism had waned but the city was still Liberal and leftward leaning within a predominantly Conservative county. The affluent days of the wool trade and weaving were long gone but the tanning of leather and the manufacture of shoes were thriving as were several substantial iron and metalwork production companies such as Boulton & Paul and Laurence, Scott and Electromotors, which shipped all over the world. Brewing, mustard, clothing and chocolate manufacture were also prominent. Several business families led the philanthropic and social progress of the city. The Colmans (strong Liberals), the Gurneys of The Bank, the Jarrolds of printing and department store fame, and the Sextons of shoes were amongst the foremost.

The old medieval heart of the city with its winding streets, its houses with over-hanging first storeys, its wide weavers' windows, its large number of medieval churches and a proliferation of pubs, was still extant. But much of it was in deep decay and was pocketed with slum housing in insanitary, overcrowded 'yards'. Outside the remnants of the old city walls were long streets of Victorian and Edwardian brick-built terraces for the generally working-class population of around 112,000. The city was governed by a Corporation.

1. The corner of St Stephen's Street and Surrey Street, Norwich circa 1910.

The Manthorpe family was new to Norwich. They had a long history in Yarmouth where they had been prominent in the mercantile class supporting Cromwell during the Civil War. After the Restoration their fortunes sank so that by the 19th century Andrew Manthorpe worked as a Longshoreman. His Mariner's Register Ticket states that he was only 5 foot 3 ½ inches in height and had brown hair and eyes and a fair complexion. His eldest son Hamilton was born in Yarmouth in 1854. Hamilton earned a certificate in free-hand drawing from the Yarmouth School of Art and was apprenticed into the trade of coach smith.

2. Model anvil and hammer that were Hamilton's apprentice pieces.

He married Eliza Land in 1876 and lived in Southtown, Great Yarmouth where their eldest children were born: Matilda (1876) and George (1878). Then in 1881 something calamitous happened—what he called mysteriously in his diary twenty-one years later a 'dark day'—perhaps the loss of a steady job, an injury, or an eviction. They moved to Diss where Anne was born in 1882 and Walter, the youngest was born in Norwich, in the parish of St Stephen's, in 1883.

According to their son Walter, writing in later life, Hamilton was a heavy-handed, tough father and his account book attests to his up-hill struggle with the daily business of earning a living. He knew he had a tendency to

3. Hamilton and Eliza Manthorpe

grumble and presumably took out his temper on the boys, but he also had a twinkle in his eye and a broad, pleasant face. For a while Hamilton worked in Chapelfield, most likely at a works near The Coachmaker's Arms public house. There was one close by run by a man named Howes. Walter attended the Avenue Road School which he remembered later as a very good school.

4. *Avenue Road School class from 1897 with teachers Miss Tennant (far left middle) and Mr Smith (far right middle). Walter is in the top row, last boy on the left.*

In the early 1890s George contracted tuberculosis, the scourge of the poor and badly housed, and his parents sent him to relatives in Yarmouth in the hope of his recovering with the sea air but he died in 1892 aged just 14. Walter would have been 9 years old. It was three years later that Hamilton and Eliza applied to join the Society of Friends. They were living at 111 Cambridge Street in what could not have been a more modest terrace house and before long they moved to an equally limited house in Newmarket Street.

Their letter of application to the Friends (1895) shows that one or both of them had been attending the Quaker adult education programme [First-Day School][12] and had become followers of a Christianity that expected 'the coming of his kingdom'.[13]

EASTERN COUNTIES' FIRST-DAY ADULT SCHOOLS.

UNITED MEETINGS,

NOVEMBER 15TH, 16TH, & 17TH, 1890.

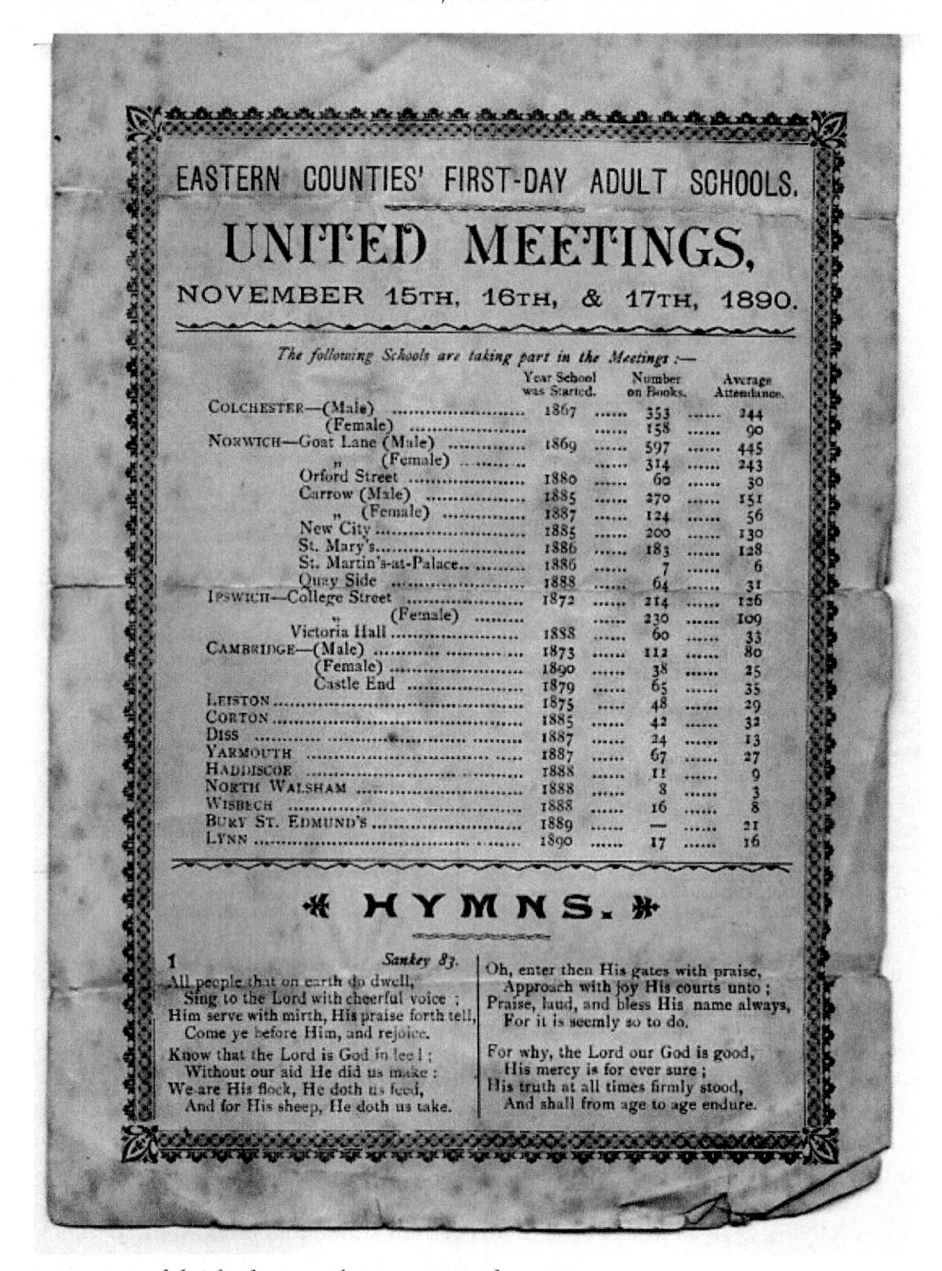

The following Schools are taking part in the Meetings:—

	Year School was Started.	Number on Books.	Average Attendance.
COLCHESTER—(Male)	1867	353	244
" (Female)		158	90
NORWICH—Goat Lane (Male)	1869	597	445
" (Female)		314	243
Orford Street	1880	60	30
Carrow (Male)	1885	270	151
" (Female)	1887	124	56
New City	1885	200	130
St. Mary's	1886	183	128
St. Martin's-at-Palace	1886	7	6
Quay Side	1888	64	31
IPSWICH—College Street	1872	214	126
" (Female)		230	109
Victoria Hall	1888	60	33
CAMBRIDGE—(Male)	1873	112	80
" (Female)	1890	38	25
Castle End	1879	65	35
LEISTON	1875	48	29
CORTON	1885	42	32
DISS	1887	24	13
YARMOUTH	1887	67	27
HADDISCOE	1888	11	9
NORTH WALSHAM	1888	8	3
WISBECH	1888	16	8
BURY ST. EDMUND'S	1889	—	21
LYNN	1890	17	16

❈ HYMNS. ❈

1 *Sankey 83.*
All people that on earth do dwell,
 Sing to the Lord with cheerful voice;
Him serve with mirth, His praise forth tell,
 Come ye before Him, and rejoice.

Know that the Lord is God in deed;
 Without our aid He did us make:
We are His flock, He doth us feed,
 And for His sheep, He doth us take.

Oh, enter then His gates with praise,
 Approach with joy His courts unto;
Praise, laud, and bless His name always,
 For it is seemly so to do.

For why, the Lord our God is good,
 His mercy is for ever sure;
His truth at all times firmly stood,
 And shall from age to age endure.

5. *First-Day Adult Schools notice of meetings November 1890.*

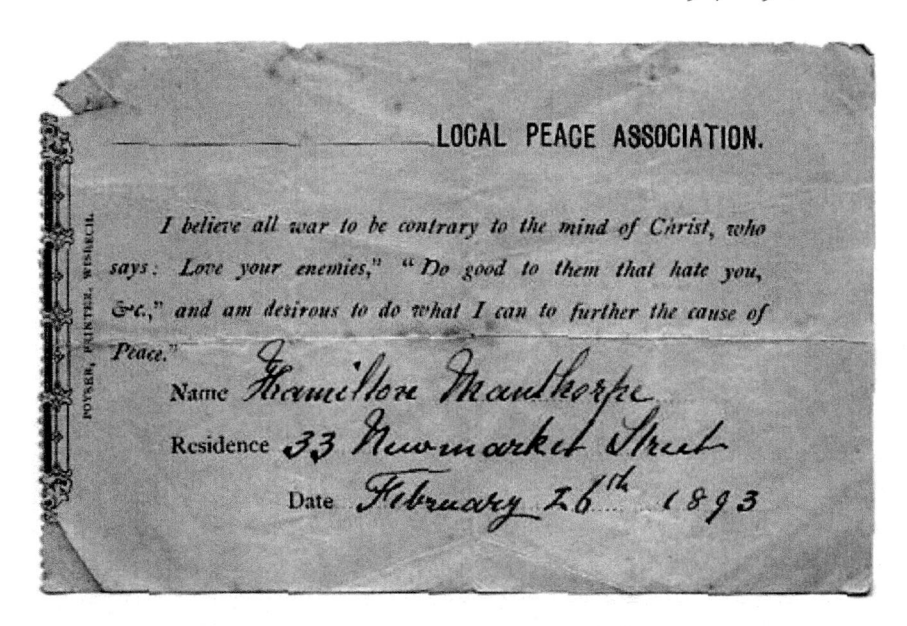

6. Hamilton's Peace Pledge 1893.

As was, and is, Quaker custom, some "weighty" (senior) Friends visited their home and interviewed them to assess the seriousness of their intent and their domestic circumstances, and the record of that judgement was inscribed in the Minutes of the Monthly Meeting of May 1895:

> We have had a satisfactory interview with Hamilton and Eliza Manthorpe. They have not hitherto been in membership with any other denomination. Eliza Manthorpe experienced conversion at an earlier period than her husband, whose definite religious convictions date from his attendance at the school about eight years ago. Though he had attended the evening Meetings, his attendance in the mornings began about three years since, and his wife followed a little later. They are both in full sympathy with us in the Christian views which distinguish us from other denominations, some of which they seem to have adopted before their acquaintance with Friends. We have confidence in recommending the monthly Meeting to accede to their application.
>
> John Howes. E.L. Sayer. Henry Brown.[14]

Both Cambridge Street and Newmarket Street are just a fifteen or twenty-minute walk from the Goat Lane Meeting House, a grandly porticoed building paid for by the affluent Gurneys; it was a far cry from some of the modest single room country meeting houses of the eighteenth century and it aptly resembles a bank.

Hamilton became involved in collecting for the Temperance movement (he himself had become teetotal) and supporting the Peace Movement within the

7. Members of the Society of Friends outside Goat Lane Meeting House, Norwich. Hamilton Manthorpe, seated on ground with legs out, front row second from left.

8. Hamilton (standing top left) with his two daughters (seated on step), Matilda and Anne outside Goat Lane Meeting House.

Meeting. He continued his attendance at the First-Day school for twenty years and eventually taught in it. Quite apart from the advantages of being supported by a religious community and developing literacy skills, the First-Day Adult School ran a modest insurance scheme to which members subscribed weekly and could draw from when ill-health, bad weather or other circumstances prevented the men from working. This would have been an absolute godsend as Hamilton was subject to the usual misfortunes of accidents and illness due to his outdoor and heavy work. For example in April 1898 he had a bad fall from the front of the van (waggon) and "called on the club". In 1900 he was unable to work at all for a full six months. As a family they were respectable working poor but nevertheless, week by week, they were within a hair's breadth of destitution. Andrew's widow, Hamilton's mother, ended up in a workhouse.

These factors alone, the tragedy of sickness due to poverty resulting in the death of his elder brother, and his father's tenuous employment and income, are enough to account for Walter's determination to pull himself out of the cycle of poverty and for him to develop an interest in health in general. Through the Quaker connections he was able to find a way.

From 1896, Hamilton was running the Quaker coffee and chocolate stall on

9. *Hamilton's coffee stall outside St Andrew's Hall, Norwich.*

St Andrew's Plain—an alternative to beer for the men heading for work at the factories around Colegate. The horse-drawn carts opened at 5 or 5.30 am and no item of food cost more than a halfpenny. His small black account book from 1896 to 1904 survives and in between the figures he wrote occasional comments, such as 23 January, 1897, "dragged anchor several yards" which refers in nautical terms to the cart getting out of control, and "weather very bad"— 20 March "great football match". Mostly the notes are about the health of family members, day trips and holidays to Yarmouth, which he often called "the old town" and regarded as home, and attending the Quarterly Quaker Meetings. In July 1898, Matilda bought a sewing machine from one of the Friends, a Mrs Copeman—the beginning of her work as a seamstress. Walter got his first long trousers the same month.

For the rest of his work Hamilton seems to have been odd-jobbing—house painting and builders work and repairing waggons where his smithing would have come into play. He also had some artistic dexterity and painted the coats of arms on the carriage doors of the gentry. He often walked long distances around Norwich and well into the country. Later he had a bicycle. When the work was forthcoming he cheered up: "a glorious week life worth living". But evidently there were very lean times when all the employment he had was the coffee cart and he several times notes: "Thank God for J.J. Cadbury", the Quaker provider of cocoa. In 1900 he started counting his blessing every week—perhaps a new practice suggested at the Meeting. He once humorously referred to himself and his wife as 'The King and Queen of Cambridge Street'. When Queen Victoria died in January 1901 he noted, "The Queen was buried on Saturday, at home all day but must confess I did not mourn."

The Census report of 1901 shows the family consisting of Walter aged 15 and already a grocer's apprentice, Matilda age 24 a tailoress, and Anne aged 19 also a tailoress.[15] And in this tiny two-up-two-down house they also had a lodger, Laura Smith, a tailoress, aged 25.

There were celebrations at Crown Point, the home of the Colman family, to mark the coronation of Edward VII in 1902 and Hamilton purveyed large amounts of tea and coffee to the crowds.[16] Trade picked up in 1902 and Hamilton noted "no illness, many outings with Quakers." The following year, from February was also good: "8 wonderful weeks, good weather, good trade, good health, good God, everything good but myself very unworthy." But by April, he was "very ill all this week, bad weather, there I am, I soon begin to grumble."

In August he took "a wet drive to Tasburgh" and went to see Mr Eddington "on behalf of my son." That was the beginning of Walter working for Mr Eddington and of the Eddingtons taking a personal interest in his development.[17] The Eddington family came from the West Country and had been Quakers for generations. Alexander had moved into business with his uncle Harry Brown also a Quaker (who had approved Hamilton and Eliza's application), of Unthank Road, Height, in Norwich in 1884. Their substantial business was Eddington grocery and tea traders on Gentleman's Walk. Edith Cavell was one of their customers. Alexander acted as a clerk of the Meeting and was a stalwart of the Society. He was known to encourage and support people whom he felt had potential. Although, theoretically the Quakers recognised no distinction between the classes, the fact that the Eddingtons were of a higher class and better educational background than the Manthorpes must certainly have helped them.

10. The staff of Eddington's on the Walk. Walter is fifth from the right.

There is no record of Walter having formally joined the Society of Friends but since he attended with his parents and then on his own account, he probably didn't have to—he was raised into the community and their ideals. The Friends' meetings provided a weekly pattern of quiet reflection, recognition of man as a spiritual being, the assertion of human equality without distinction of class, nationality, race or sex and encouraged moral education through debate. Unfortunately, despite the example of Elizabeth Fry, there was still a strong bias towards patriarchy - women did not attend the business meetings unless there was a specific point of reference to their activities. Nevertheless, Walter would have learned to value discourse and to make considered decisions. At its best, Christianity provides a moral and social education. Within the limitations of his economic background, Walter had an active and intelligent mind. In later years he recalled the educational value of Quakerism:

The Adult School Movement was a very great success in Norwich. It was early on Sunday. It began at 9 o'clock on Sunday morning. There was quite a large number of men who joined the Adult School. All those who gave their activities to the Adult School, did so as a kind of .... without any kind of remuneration. They did it freely of themselves. It was really a wonderful moment. And one of the great disasters of the war was the killing of the Adult School Movement. That killed it. The War did

It was a question of the Bible being read to start off with and the time that one was there was spent discussing what had been read in the Bible. That was what the Adult School Movement was. And there were different kinds of institutions set up like - ere - Sailors Club which was part of it and which was helpful to people.[18]

In addition to this mental and moral training, the Friends provided another essential ingredient in his development. Walter was a keen athlete especially in gymnastics, rowing and football. He became a member of the Boy's Brigade commanded by Eddington, which although it had the trappings of a corps, had no military intention. It was a precursor of the Boy Scouts, and founded by Sir William Alexander Smith Of Thurso, Scotland. The Brigade's motto was "Sure and Steadfast" and the aim was "The advancement of Christ's kingdom among boys and the promotion of habits of Obedience, Reverence, Discipline, Self-respect and all that tends towards a true Christian manliness."

11. Boys' Life Brigade 1910. Location in Norwich unknown.
Mr Todd — Captain; Walter Manthorpe — Lieutenant; Mr Girling — Bandmaster; Mr Thompson (far right) — First-Aid Instructor (a fire engine driver for the Police Fire Brigade); AJ Eddington; PJ Boddy; and J Papps - in civilian clothes.

Activities included first-aid, swimming and lifesaving, camping and a band. Walter was also very keen on hockey and gymnastics.

12. A mixed hockey team at Westfield, Eaton Village. Walter middle row, centre left.

By 1911, the Census shows Hamilton and Eliza living at 51 Connaught Road, Norwich—a tiny terrace house off the Dereham Road, with Walter now aged 25. Around this time it seems that Walter took an interest in the 'lodging house mission' Dorothy Jewson's pioneering study of *"The destitute of Norwich and how they live"*[19].

The family used nicknames for each other; Hamilton was Hammy, Eliza was Fubsy, Anne was Tubsy, Matilda was Matchstick and Walter was Posh but although living so closely together, they were not demonstrative in their

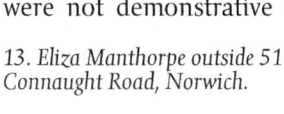

13. Eliza Manthorpe outside 51 Connaught Road, Norwich.

affections. Despite hardships, life seems to have been easing up a little since Walter had time for sports and occasional excursions that wouldn't have been available to his parents.

After he had finished his apprenticeship Walter continued to work for Eddington's as a shop assistant where the practical ethics of Quakerism would have been played out in the transactions of daily life—every interaction has a moral responsibility. But something had got into Walter that made him rather different. As he wrote fifty years later, he had become inspired:

14. Walter (left) with Arthur Breeze camping at Whitlingham. Interesting to see the gun in the foreground; were they copying the style of the safari or camping expedition? Arthur Breeze died in 1918.

> If I consider what lit the fire of enthusiasm in me in taking a step which was entirely against my employers [sic] advice, it would be difficult to pinpoint. But with the arrival of magazines from America edited by Bernarr [sic] McFadden what I read in them added fuel to my imagination and practicality to the beliefs I already had.[20]

MacFadden was a bodybuilder and founded *Physical Culture* magazine in 1899. He introduced the term *Nature Cure* and promoted fasting, natural health, vegetarian diet and natural views on sex (that sex was not solely for procreation). Walter was smitten and so, with only £25 capital, he decided to open his own Health Food Store which in those days meant selling molasses, honey, dried fruits and nuts, olive oil, wholemeal flour and other grains—and above all wholemeal bread.[21] He opened his shop in 1913 at rented premises at 8 White Lion Street then, and now, a modest little street but just round the corner from Gentleman's Walk. He was one of a very few such proprietors in the country and one of the earliest in the provinces.

> I had served four years as an apprentice and taken a great interest in food itself that was one of the basic reasons of why I took a health food stores even at that time there was a lot of controversy over as to what food contained and idea of a health food stores was that foods only should be sold without an excess of chemicals. Perhaps the most important thing of the day and now is the question of bread and the honest local bread is a hundred percent whole wheat containing the germ and the bran and so. And that's just an important question today and its things of that kind that interested me at that time.[22]

What we now take for granted was then, and for many decades, off beat, cranky, even tinged with the visionary. Walter gave up eating meat and became a lifelong vegetarian and advocated a new conviction: that good health could be encouraged and sustained by the quality of the foods you eat.[23] Good food meant unrefined grains and unadulterated pure ingredients from known sources. In time he knew not only where his honey came from in England, but also where the best oases for dates were in North Africa.

15. Walter Manthorpe outside his shop in White Lion Street, Norwich 1914.

Many years later I heard the local reaction to this new enterprise from old Mr Bartram of Bartram Mowers who recalled the opening of Walter's shop. He told me *"We thought it would be a nine-day wonder"*. Such was the scepticism of the time but as we now know, over the twentieth century, diet and healthy eating have become a kind of secular religion.

The shop on White Lion Street, leased from another Quaker, Thomas Copeman[24] was very plain —just the one room on the ground floor and two floors above for packing up the dry goods, plus a damp basement. Walter's best assets were his passionate convictions about health and whole food, his own athletic health, and his willingness to advise his customers on diet. He was teaching himself from a collection of books he was building up on the subject. But fortuitously, it was not just a new career that beckoned, he was also enamoured of a young woman called Jane Swann who worked in a Norwich confectionery shop, Ladells, and had retail experience.

They were both aged 30 when they married in May 1915 and they honeymooned in the Lake District. Jane was not a Quaker but a member of the Church of England; she came from a farming family originally from Worstead, north west of Norwich, but latterly from Lakenham.[25] As a couple Walter and Jane compromised on matters of faith and attended the Congregational church on Princes Street. They were totally invested in the potential of the new business and ready to start a family on their prospects. They moved into a terraced house at 47 Trafford Road, then on the edge of Norwich, where they both remained for the rest of their lives. Their first child, little Walter, was born in November 1916. But the early years were financially very hard going indeed and had it not been for loyal customers it's hard to see how they would have survived. During this period, perhaps as part of their Christian witness, and perhaps there was some stipend, they took in a family of Belgian refugees and housed them in an upper floor of the shop.

16. *Jane Swann*

Notes

1. Gregory, Adrian. *The Last Great War. British Society and the First World War*, 2008, pp.16–17.
2. Others were less optimistic even from the beginning, including the Prime Minister, Herbert Asquith who foresaw Armageddon.
3. *Eastern Daily Press*, 3 August 1914.
4. Browning, Stephen. *Norwich in the Great War*, 2015, p. 38.
5. Gregory, p. 75. R.H. Mottram's *The Window Seat or Life Observed*, 1954, chapter 31 gives a picture of Norwich at this time.
6. Browning, p. 27.
7. It was Derby who had come up with what now, with the benefit of hindsight, seems like a bad joke, the idea of "Pals".
8. Gregory, p. 89, "It needs to be remembered that the vast majority of the men of military age in Britain during the First World War chose not to volunteer for the armed forces."

9. Canvassing for registration was carried out entirely by volunteers, mostly middle-aged men. Gregory, p. 93.
10. Gregory, p. 91.
11. Ceadel, p. 45. Ceadal calls the Bloomsbury objectors 'quasi-pacifist' because of their reliance on influence and privilege.
12. The First Day [Sunday] Adult School movement was set up by the Quaker Rowntree family to address the educational, social and religious needs of the poor and to teach them how to apply the lessons of Christianity to everyday life.
13. Letter in possession of the author signed by Hamilton and Eliza Manthorpe.
14. NRO/SF62. P434. Henry Brown was in partnership with Arthur Eddington. It's possible that this Howes was the coachmaker.
15. Reel 1 Imperial War Museum interview tapes: *"I left school at fourteen and I served four years apprenticeship to a grocery business in the City and the difference in wages between then and now is almost unbelievable."*
16. 3 1/2 urns of tea. 1 ¾ urns of coffee. 37 gross of Buns, 124 doz ginger beer. Takings £20.2.0
17. Interview in the EDP 1970s, age 79. "Over the Tea table". "Mr Manthorpe began working as a lad with Underhills and then moved next door but one with Alexander Eddington. His interest in athletics, football and rowing led him to reading widely on the subject of food and health."
18. Reel 3, IWM tapes.
19. Dorothy Jewson was a trade union organiser and later a Labour party politician so this indicates Walter's social and political perspective at the time. His involvement is indicated, but not confirmed, in a newspaper cutting amongst his papers.
20. From *"Fifty Years in Health Food"* in *"The Health Food Trader"* magazine No 53 Nov 1964.
21. His sister Matilda had married Arthur Jermy and moved to Bradford where Walter went to visit her. It's possible that it was in Bradford that he first saw a health food shop—there was one at 1096 Manchester Road.
22. Reel 1, IWM tapes.
23. Family legend has it that before he renounced meat he ate a whole goose.
24. The Copemans were a well-known Quaker and business family in Norwich and one of the founders of the *Eastern Daily Press*.
25. Her father Walter Swann was listed as a Post Office sorting clerk, living in 1901 at 60 Ashby Street, Norwich and lately moved to King's Road, Lakenham Norwich.

2. 1916–February 1917

There were many reasons to oppose the war: political, religious and intellectual, and variations within those categories. Right from the beginning, Keir Hardie, the founder of the Labour Party, spoke out publicly against it. Men committed to International Socialism objected to waging war on their fellow workers in other countries, considering that the real enemy was the ruling classes who had inflicted this conflict upon them. The problem was that they needed to gain the co-operation of their French and German counterparts to stage pan-European strike action to sabotage the war and that co-operation was not forthcoming.[1]

Religious objection was strongest amongst Protestant non-conformists with varying degrees of resistance. Plymouth Brethren or Seventh Day Adventists, for example, were likely to be Absolutists who would not co-operate in any way whatsoever, while Methodists and Quakers might join an Ambulance Unit or the Non-Combatant Corps. The Society of Friends held a strong position of credibility because of its commitment to non-violence since the 1660s but also because of its shift from an outlawed faction in the seventeenth century to an influential sect in the nineteenth, wielding its moral leadership in business, banking, social reform and philanthropy. A few Anglican clergy spoke out against the war but most either acquiesced or positively supported it, many quite vehemently, from the pulpit.[2]

Of the intellectuals and artists who simply opposed the savagery of war, the philosopher Bertrand Russell had the highest public profile, with the out-spoken George Bernard Shaw and many of the Bloomsbury Group of artists and writers actively resisting. Class played a very important part in how you were treated: Bertrand Russell, the second son of an Earl, was imprisoned (for sedition) but provided with the comforts thought to be necessary for a gentleman. Some members of the Bloomsbury Group evaded conscription by renting farms and thus becoming 'necessary' to the war effort.[3]

One thing seems clear, that those who chose the route of conscientious objection, whether for political or religious reasons, were strong individualists. They were mentally capable of framing their position and their argument and of sufficient self-composure and conviction to resist the pressures of public opinion, bearing in mind that in the days before general use of telephone, car travel or electric light, local communities were tight knit and people were very dependent on each other. Because they had strong personalities, conscientious objectors (COs) argued among themselves as well as with everyone else. Some socialists and anarchists had no objection to violence per se but wouldn't take on this particular quarrel. For those who had extreme religious views and were waiting for Christ's Second Coming, the war was an irrelevance, a distraction. The diversity of opinions worked both for and against those who identified as conscientious objectors: they had no unified opposition to the government but then the government found it hard to find a single policy to deal with them. Generally speaking, it was the established bodies of Quakerism, Methodism and the Independent Labour Party (ILP) that gave COs their support and publicised their plights.

Early on in the war, national organizations were set up specifically to support conscientious objectors, the most notable being the No-Conscription Fellowship (NCF) led by Fenner Brockway and Clifford Allen, both socialist politicians. Catherine Marshall covertly produced its illicit journal called *The Tribunal* which was crucial in keeping the anti-war issue alive. Most members of the NCF were either ILP Socialists or Quakers. In anticipation of the arrest of their key activists, they ensured continuity by having shadow or back-up personnel for the key roles, using the models developed by the Suffragettes and Sinn Fein. They campaigned against conscription, circulated information and provided active support to COs and their families.[4]

Provincially and locally, Quakers maintained the opposition in a lower key. From the Minute Book of the Norwich Society of Friends, there is a note of a talk about 'The Peace Question' in October 1914, although what that talk was, the minute does not say. By November, Norwich Friends were making clothes for Belgian refugees. In January 1915 the entry says: 'Particulars have been given of work for the Belgians, Germans, Friends Ambulance Unit, and Friends' War Victims Fund and the Red Cross by the workers in Norwich, the Civil Club, and by Friends of Pakefield[5]; also about £7 has been collected by those appointed at the last meeting.'

On 10 February, Edward H. Kemp and A. Fisher resigned from the Meeting because they had joined the army. Their resignation was not immediately accepted and the Clerk (A Eddington) recorded the following minute:

> We, most of us at least, feel that this awful war has emphasized (sic) the sinfulness and folly of all war and of preparation for war, and that it must be contrary to the mind of Christ; at the same time we would not judge those who think otherwise and that it is the duty of England to defend a weak nation [i.e. Belgium], and of her Citizens to train and take arms to defend her own shores. Therefore whilst thanking the above named Friends for their straight forward action, we think it may be the right course, with all the uncertainties of the future before us, to leave the consideration of the subject for the present, say until 6 months after the conclusion of the peace. We trust our Friends will be willing to concur to this view of the matter.

But E.H. Kemp was determined to resign on the basis that 'a soldier cannot be a Quaker'.

In May 1915, Matilda Jermy, Walter's sister, applied for membership to the

17. *Matilda Jermy née Manthorpe, who actively supported her brother's pacifism.*

Norwich Meeting. She had been attending meetings since the age of 16 but her marriage to Arthur R. Jermy had failed and she had returned from Bradford to Norwich alone.[6] After being interviewed by several Friends she was accepted into the meeting in June and by March of the following year was appointed to the Library Committee.

There was a collection for the Victims of War, and Percy J. Boddy[7] was appointed Correspondent with the Friends Home Mission, an outreach initiative:

> May 1915
>
> This meeting has had concern brought before it under the feeling that it is very undesirable at the present time to have a discussion at the Yearly Meeting on the action of Friends who are serving in the Army — partly these Friends will be unavoidably absent, but still more because such discussion would probably be more profitable when the war is over. AE [A. Eddington]

In November 1915 it was noted that "Several have spoken of the efforts being made to induce young men to join the army." This presumably didn't sit well with the Friends and two months later they took a more definite step:

> January 1916
>
> Letters have been received from the Friends' Service Committee and the Secretary of the local No-Conscription Fellowship. This meeting feels strongly the unlawfulness of taking human life, and whilst not binding ourselves to any course of action, we appoint James Riches as our representative to keep in touch with the No-Conscription Fellowship.

At this point COs were still being dealt with under military law and the minute from the July 1916 Meeting, Item 8 states that:

> D. Casseretto has given an account of the Free Church Meeting[8] from which a Petition was sent to the Government asking that all Conscientious Objectors should be handed over to the Civil Authority.

Nationally, the estimates for the numbers of men applying for conscientious objector status varies from 14,000 to 19,000, and resting at around 16,000. Although the Peace Pledge Union on its website gives the figures of 1,500 imprisoned, 13,000 doing work of national importance and 5,000 in the Non-Combatant Brigade, but there may have been some movement between these groups.[9]

Those who refused to go through the process for exemption, or if their case was rejected, were still subject to conscription and had either to join the military or be subject to a military court martial. There are numerous examples of men who found themselves in the army and then refused to comply with military demands, even down to refusing to don the uniform, and were subject to cruel and abusive detentions.[10] Some were tortured and even threatened with execution but this was widely publicised and resulted in a public outcry and rescinding of the sentences. What, after all, were the soldiers fighting for if not freedom from a militaristic state?

The government was not about to change its tune but, in the interest of public relations, it had to modify the worst effects of its policy towards COs, especially as numbers were growing and the army was fed up with trying to deal with them.[11] The Pelham Committee had been set up under the auspices of the Board of Trade in March 1916 to enable conditionally exempted men to find work of National Importance. But there was a gap between those men, and the Absolutist conscientious objectors who would stay in prison through the war. In this gap were the Alternativists, men who refused compulsory non-military service in the Non-Combatant Corps. These men were court-martialled and imprisoned. It was large numbers of these men who were rapidly filling up the prisons so that by August 1916 it became necessary to find other suitable placements. The Home Office was instructed to set up a committee under chairmanship of William Brace, a pro-war Welsh Labour MP to resolve the issue. Despite its Home Office umbrella, it was comprised largely of retired military men with little or no sympathy for COs.

The result was that men who had been handed over to the military were returned to civilian control. Those 'genuine' objectors, those with real ethical and spiritual objections as opposed to those trying to evade conscription, would be given the chance to do work 'of national importance' under what became known as the Home Office Scheme. Since many private firms wouldn't employ COs, either from personal distaste or from fear that they might affect the rest of the work force, this work would take place in specially created work camps and prisons redesignated for the purpose.[12] Those who refused even this outlet would continue in prison. This new Scheme potentially divided the objectors into those of rigid conscience who were willing to take the toughest stance and stay in prison—the Absolutists—and those who opted for the 'easier' option – Alternativists. However, it was recognised that older and married men risked losing their families and being unable to contribute anything towards their upkeep if they did not take the Home Office option. Later the NCF gave its full support to the 'Schemers'.

In August the Minutes of the Norwich Meeting of the Society of Friends noted that they had purchased a copy of the book *The Last Weapon*[13], a dystopian novel, and that "Much interesting information has been given us respecting some of our members and others who are Conscientious Objectors".

In November 1916 the Meeting "Received a deputation from the Peace Negotiations Society." And in May the following year the same Peace Negotiations Society asked for use of the Meeting House but it was 'hoped that the Meeting will not be advertised in the newspapers.' One wonders if they feared public reaction. During his interview with the Imperial War Museum in 1974, Walter remembered that the Society of Friends already had a strong national network of Meetings and that helped support the objectors' views.[14] He had certainly made up his mind early on — even before the war started — that he was opposed to the killing of humans and animals. He had also had plenty of time to learn about what was happening to other COs:[15]

> Personally, I had decided when the war was first talked about that I should be a CO. I decided from the very start. It wasn't something I made up my mind you know after conditions. It was on the question of war itself that I decided to be a CO. I disagreed with war itself as not being an answer to the problem. That was my attitude.[16]

It seems, from a newspaper interview he gave in later years, that Walter was arrested more than once.[17] Without specific evidence my guess is that on the first occasion—or perhaps there were more—he was arrested and then released. The Norwich Tribunals were held on Wednesdays and reported in the *Eastern Daily Press* on Thursdays but only the more interesting cases were noted.

Looking back from 1974 Walter remembered that he was willing to discuss his point of view if it came up but "there wasn't very much occasion for people to be able to discuss these things at that time. The men who joined the army they simply just accepted it and so and if you became a CO you more or less under took that to a large extent. And it had to be placed as a decision of your own."[18] Neither did he think he had read much about pacifism—being guided entirely by the Bible.[19] He was aware of the NCF and the Fellowship of Reconciliation[20] activities going on in London but said that he had no opportunity to come in contact with those people. However, in his statement of defence in 1917 he stated that he was a member of the Norwich Local Peace Movement and took part in their activities, so, by 1974, time had dulled his memory. He did remember that there was considerable pressure from society as a whole to join up and that among his friends very few understood his position and, in any case, they had been called up.[21] He was never given a white feather, but outside of the Meeting House and his family, his position was isolated.[22]

Tribunals had been created by the 1916 Military Service Act and were overseen by the Local Government Board. They were the same tribunals that had been set up to deal with applications for delayed military service under the 'Derby' Scheme for people who were not opposed to the war, but had valid reasons for resisting conscription, such as being relied upon by helpless dependents or having jobs that were of national importance. This latter category tended naturally to favour the educated professional classes leaving the lower classes to fend for themselves. The cases for conscientious objectors were simply added to the tribunals workload. These tribunals were run by local worthies and magistrates, members of the establishment, and with the addition of the CO cases their objectives were confused if not conflicted. The War Office paid their expenses and supplied

Military Representatives to make the case for the army who might also retire with the committee to take a decision.[23] The recommendations of the local tribunals were then sent on to the Central Tribunal in London which would give the final adjudication.

Most of the records of tribunals were destroyed by the government in the early 1920s on the basis that the material was 'sensitive'.[24] There are just a few remaining as result of accident or oversight. However, John William Graham in his book *Conscription and Conscience A History 1916-1919* which was written in 1922 is an excellent source of first-hand accounts of the experience of COs at tribunals.[25] The boards were given the task of assessing the validity of men's spiritual experience or, in the case of the Independent Labour Party, their political views. Yet they had no proper training or guidelines to do this, and often were not even educated in the basic tenants of Christianity. Moreover, many of those who sat on tribunals unashamedly expressed blatant political and religious prejudices. Everything was weighted towards conscription. Nor was there any uniformity of approach in discernment. The quality of a tribunal varied from place to place, and some were known to be much harsher than others. The hope of anything like a fair hearing was slight. Many, if not most, of the young—and they were often very young—men coming before them were working class or lower middle class and had no experience of standing up to their elders or 'betters'. Class was a very potent instrument of discrimination, taken for granted as a norm and rarely questioned.

The COs were by and large extremely upstanding people, it went with the religious territory, so that the very fact of finding themselves in police court was daunting and shaming. They knew they were going to be treated like criminals and actually criminalised. For many of them their stance would mean complete rejection by their families and ostracism from their friends, although this was not the case for Quakers.

By 1917, Kitchener had been killed, the first and bloodiest Battle of the Somme had been fought and Lloyd George had become prime minister. The country was desperately short of recruits. In January of 1917 it was reported in the *Eastern Daily Press* (EDP) that The Local Government Board had decided that after 31 January every man under the age of 31 who was fit for military service or for garrison service abroad would be deemed more useful in the forces than in civil employment, except for those certified categories already identified.[26] This tightened the net and gave tribunals less room for manoeuvre with regard to exemptions. The *EDP* followed up with an editorial on 23 January supporting the measures and the war effort. A boot and shoe firm had applied for exemption for sixty-six of its workers[27] but the military applied for withdrawal of exemption certificates for fifty-four of the men. At the same tribunal, the tensions between city and county were shown by the attempt of Lord Kimberley, Chairman of the Norfolk Appeal Tribunal, to interfere in the Norwich decisions with regard to agricultural exemptions and the special cases of horsemen.[28] He was roundly rebuffed.[29] Further, the *EDP* reported at the end of February that the army wanted men to train up over the summer and that "over a 1,000 men were wanted out of the City of Norwich in the next fortnight or three weeks."[30] The pressure was on.

It was at this point, early in 1917, two and half years into the war, that Walter was taken before the local tribunal in the Police Court at the Guildhall in Norwich, just beside the market place. This was the preliminary tribunal. The Norwich Tribunal consisted of ten men (no women) chosen by the City Council: Alderman Ernest Blyth, Alderman George Henry Morse (brewer), Alderman James Baxter (timber merchant), Councillor Richard Winsor Bishop (jeweller), Councillor Fredrick Bassingthwaite (baker and grocer), Dr John Griffiths-Mann (doctor), Edmund Reeve (solicitor) and Alfred Water (printer). Frank Meeres, in his book *Norfolk in the First World War*, points out that Herbert Witard, an alderman who was against the war, was denied a place on the committee.[31] The President of the Tribunal was Alderman Blyth[32] and the military representative was Major J.A. Berners.

The brisk style of Major Berners is indicated from his interrogation of a Dr Watson, a timber merchant and partner in a market gardening business, who sought exemption. Major Berners asked if growing tomatoes and asparagus was in the national interest and upon being told that tomatoes were popular in Manchester, he replied "I never eat them; and as for asparagus we can all do without that."[33]

Dr Blyth (1857-1934) was a native of Norwich, a Baptist and a solicitor. He was an ardent educationalist, at various times chairman of the governors of the Norwich School, the City of Norwich School, Notre Dame School and later the Blyth School. He was a Trustee of the Norwich Protestant Dissenters Benevolent Association. He was an alderman, mayor and later Lord Mayor and undoubtedly part of the establishment of Norwich.[34]

The *EDP* reported on 31 January that two conscientious objectors were sent for non-combatant service, they were not named but it is almost certain that these two were Walter Manthorpe and Jack Ashley[35] since they were both in Britannia Barracks by 12 February and the next EDP report on the Local Tribunal on 7 February makes no mention of COs.

Typically, for both Norwich as a quiet provincial town, and for my grandfather as one who organised his own affairs, the timing of his arrest seems to have been a matter of mutual agreement:

> Because ... having a public business I was fairly well known to the police and consequently ... instead of there being an arrest it was a question of meeting the police at a certain time. That's what that came to. I agreed to that. There was no compulsion about it.[36]

Fortunately for him, the Quakers supported him and Mrs Florence Eddington herself attended the hearing although even sixty years later, out of courteous reticence, Walter was unwilling to name her.[37] Walter's verbal defence was no more or less than his written Defence. As he explained:

> You had nothing else to say, you see. You were there because you did not accept an order, or demand, to what you should do. You resisted that and the reason why you resisted that was because of these principles you see. That's the only thing you can do.[38]

It's unlikely by this time that he hoped to be fully exempted, and he was not. He was sent to the military barracks at Mousehold on the north east edge of Norwich, which in itself was quite shameful:

> Well, the reaction was very difficult. Because to be sent to prison was looked upon at that time as one of a kind of punishment that a person of not very good intent because you broke the law and to break the law was not a thing that should be done and the conditions were that your reactions were that you were placed on a very low level, that's what it came to.[39]

On 12 February 1917 in a document headed Britannia Barracks, Walter wrote out his Defence for his court martial:

> Gentlemen
>
> My defence is that I am not a soldier, I have never taken no oath nor accepted any money. I cannot accept the position of a soldier by the operation of an act of Parliament. My non acceptance of an order is not because of antagonism to the persons concerned but to the organisation the persons represent. My reasons are that the army and its organisation exists for killing. The killing of men is entirely against my religious and moral conception of duty. I maintain, and have done so from my teens that to kill under any circumstances is a crime against the Creator. I am a believer in the individual right of man to chose [sic] his own destiny. I stand for pacifism, by that I mean actual pacifism as a practical proposition and policy. I am assured of its ultimate success. The position of this country, the bloodshed, the anxiety and the misery is the outcome of those who contribute to the policy of force. Those whose belief is founded upon carnal weapons. All religious and moral testimony is against this.
>
> I do not wish to use the Bible in my defence other than to state that the majority of true believers in its precepts cannot accept force individually and collectively as a mandate of the Prince of Peace. My upbringing from childhood has been with the Society of Friends to whose meetings I was introduced at an early age my parents who were and are now members. My appeal before the Tribunals on conscientious grounds have been

18. Interior of Norwich Prison Hall.

nullified because only recognition has been given to my business and domestic affairs, although I have pleaded for the lawful consideration on this grounds.

The military service act recognises as conscientious objection, the tribunal in principle do not.

I have been a member of the Norwich Local Peace Association and took part in activities connected with it. From 1900-1913 I was interested in an organisation whose aims and objects were the saving of life and the teaching of human brotherhood. In June 1914 I instituted a stores for the supplying of non-animal foods this being the outcome of beliefs I hold as to the right of life, the acceptance of the sanctity of life both human and animal. I maintain and will hold at whatever cost the principles here stated believing that God having made man in His image, it is not right or true policy to contribute toward the killing of men.[40]

Two important points come out of this testimony: that he had asked for, and believed that he had the right to, exemption as a conscientious objector under the Military Service Act, and, secondly, his objection was not simply on religious grounds. He did not want to use the Bible as his authority. Although he believed that Christ was the Prince of Peace he also called up a more general and political principal in his defence, he was *"a believer in the individual right of man to chose his own destiny"*. He saw himself in the tradition of liberal individualism, the individual having a moral worth and in charge of her/his own self-realisation and liberty (as opposed to collectivism or totalitarianism). Michael Ceadel makes the subtle point that by the late 19th century Liberal non-conformists had been accepted into society and lost the sense of alienation that justified and fired their position. Now, opposition to war and conscription restored that 'moral' sense to them.[41]

Walter had to supply two references and one of them, from Herbert Duncan, a Gentlemen's Mercer of 75 Upper St Giles, has survived. Duncan had known Walter for twelve years and confirmed his longstanding opposition to war and killing.[42] Indeed his reputation in Norwich seems to have been quite solid. Theo Scott, son of Augustus Frederic Scott (known as Fred), a Norwich architect and vegetarian, wrote home from the Front on 25 February 1917: "I am sorry to hear about Manthorpe [,] will his wife keep the shop on I wonder. It seems very foolish of the boards [tribunal] because I sh. [should] have put him down as a very genuine conscientious chap but errors do arise."[43]

Walter was kept at the military prison for about a month and he remembered that conditions were very similar to any other prison—very little exercise or liberty of any kind. "One thing I remember was that you had no lights and you had not lights on at any time. They certainly were severe conditions. What I remember of them."[44] Apparently the authorities hoped that the harsh conditions would change some prisoners' minds but Walter didn't come across anyone who did. It was while he was there that he faced a military court martial that was to decide his future. On 13 February 1917, he wrote to his sister Matilda, known as Tilly, what is evidently a letter designed to forestall any worry from his family:

> I feel quite satisfied that this is my truest course and this is more and more dawning on me. My time here is going all too quickly and have not yet had a dull moment. Ashley [Jack Ashley, of whom more later] and I get on A1. We don't agree of course not and this makes things all the more interesting... Our CM [Court Martial] yesterday was somewhat of a test but we have no room for fear just now there is too great a pleasure in knowing that you are given such an opportunity. We eat well sleep well and jaw well especially the latter. I have not yet decided about the H.O. [Home Office Scheme] and shall leave it till some future time there is plenty of time for this.[45]

In fact the Court Martial must have been quite a gruelling experience:

> After being in a cell I was brought before the military commanders and after my substantiating my anti-war principles I was brought out before all the troops that were stationed there and sentenced to five years penal servitude. To this I made an appeal that was not accepted and was sent to Wormwood Scrubs.[46]

This was a severe sentence and must have been a great blow. He may have had support from the Quakers and his family but, crucially, Jennie, his new wife, the mother of his five-month-old son, did not entirely agree with his position, although she understood it. But as he pointed out in 1974 it was not really a matter that was up for discussion since he had made up his mind:

> As far as the wife was concerned...she didn't have a strong idea that the only thing we should do is to join in the war, because generally speaking with all due respect to women, there are very few of them really in favour of what we know of as war.[47]

But, of course, she was going to be substantially affected by the economic and social consequences of his stance.

Notes

1. Gregory, p. 33. Differences over World War I led to the Second International being dissolved in 1916. Wikipedia *https://en.wikipedia.org/wiki/Second International* 25/06/2021
2. The vicar of St Peter Mancroft in central Norwich was a case in point. See Browning, *Norwich in the Great War*, p. 31.
3. Ceadel, p. 45 called them quasi-Pacifists.
4. Bibbings, Lois S. *Telling Tales About Men*, 2009, p. 41.
5. A Meeting near Lowestoft.

6. Letter from WM 1945—he called it a 'so-called marriage'.
7. Percy J. Boddy joined the Ambulance Unit but found it too much attached to military purposes and resigned, spending a total of two and half years in prison. Later he became Labour councillor and Sherriff of Norwich. See *htttps://www.bbc.co.uk/programmes/p02b92qf*, accessed 17/06/21.
8. The Free Church of England is an evangelical Christian church in the Anglican tradition founded in the 19th century in reaction to Anglo-Catholicism.
9. *https://menwhosaidno.org/*, accessed 12/4/21.
10. Reel 5, IWM tapes: Q. Did you ever hear any of the COs who were sent to France instead of prison. A. No I didn't know. I heard about them. I heard about men who were sent to France and whether they liked it or not they were sent out to meet the enemy but they wouldn't fire their gun or anything of that kinds. They wouldn't use the rifles that they got. No, I heard about that. The only way in which they could be sentenced out there was if they refused orders, if they refused orders then there was the possibility they would be shot. They had to do it there. It was a man who refused orders..
11. Lloyd George is quoted as saying, "I shall only consider the best means of making the path of that class [of COs] very hard one."
12. Initially Dartmoor, Wakefield and Warwick. The existing prisoners were given the opportunity to join the army at the Western Front.. It was thought that those of a violent disposition would make good soldiers. *https://academic.oup.com/histres/article/94/265/578/6285651*, accessed 20/02/23.
13. *The Last Weapon: a vision* by Theodora Wilson Wilson (sic) who was a member of the Plymouth Brethren, but from Quaker roots and returned to that faith in mid-life. In 1915 she was a founder member of the Women's International League for Peace and Freedom, a multinational group of women who campaigned to end World War I, and are still active today.
14. Reel 1, IWM tapes.
15. Ibid.
16. Ibid.
17. From an interview in an article in the *EDP*, 3 January, 1979.
18. Reel 2, IWM tapes.
19. Ibid.
20. An international movement formed in 1914 by a Quaker and a Lutheran at a Christian pacifist conference.
21. Gregory makes the point that the government was happy to deflect public discontent at food rationing and for resentment at the high level of avoidance of conscription numbers in rural areas towards COs, p. 122.
22. Reel 2, IWM tapes.
23. Bibbings, pp. 30/31.
24. Gregory, p. 101.
25. John William Graham, mathematician, writer and a significant Quaker activist (1859-1932)
26. *EDP* Microfiche 22/1/17, p. 8.
27. *EDP* 1/2/17
28. Presumably to allow for spring ploughing or sowing.
29. *EDP* 8/2/17, p. 8.
30. *EDP* 1/3/17 Report on Local Tribunals, p. 4.

31. Meeres, Frank. *Norfolk in the First World War*, 2004.
32. Ernest Egbert Blyth (1857–1934), Last Mayor & First Lord Mayor of Norwich (1910).
33. EDP 15/2/17 Norwich Tribunal report, p. 3
34. Patrick Palgrave-Moore. *The Mayors and Lord Mayors of Norwich 1836-1974*, 1978.
35. John Leonard Ashley of 120 Churchill Road, Norwich—a Congregationalist imprisoned in 1916.
36. Reel 3, IWM tapes.
37. Reel 2, IWM tapes.
38. Ibid.
39. Ibid.
40. Transcript of a handwritten 3-page document in the possession of the author.
41. Ceadel, p. 25.
42. Handwritten letter in the possession of the author dated 23 January, 1917. This letter appears to be part of his defence.
43. Letter in the possession of Judith Merrill, a great-granddaughter of Augustus Frederic Scott.
44. Reel 4, IWM tapes.
45. Letter 1, 13 February, 1917.
46. From an account he wrote for a clergyman many years later.
47. Reel 3, IWM tapes.

3. Spring 1917

Sometime in March 1917 Walter was taken, presumably frogmarched, from Mousehold the short distance down to Thorpe railway station in Norwich. He was handcuffed to a military policeman and was heading for Wormwood Scrubs. This would be his first visit to London. His mother and his sister Tilly were at the station to see him off.[1]

19. Wormwood Scrubs circa 1917.

At this point despite having been in Britannia Barracks for about four weeks, he would probably have still been reasonably fit and healthy. He now had the designation Private Walter Manthorpe since, under the Conscription Act, he was considered to have been recruited into the army. He was under military arrest because he had refused to obey orders—that is to co-operate with the army for non-combatant service, but he was being taken to a civilian prison because he identified as a conscientious objector.

All COs were imprisoned at 'third division' which meant hard labour with the first month in solitary confinement. A typical cell was ten foot long by 4 foot wide with a hard bed and night stand. Exercise was limited to walking round a yard in a circle for half an hour a day. The distance between men was exactly 8 feet and no communication was allowed.[2] Any infringements resulted in bread and water rations sometimes for months at a time. Fenner Brockway recorded that he

20. A comic postcard from Wormwood Scrubs.

was given three months bread and water until his health suffered so badly that a doctor put a stop to it.[3] Prisoners could not receive any letters for the first month. Isolation was almost total. Interestingly Walter related in a letter from 1961 that he and Richard Ashley managed to communicate

> …by means of messages passed to each other as talking was not allowed, we had devised pin pricked words on lavatory paper with the idea of encouraging each other and this had to be done without being seen by the warders who continually paraded outside the cells and could see the prisoners through a spy hole in the door both night and day.[4]

The first opportunity for Walter to tell anyone what was happening to him came many weeks after his arrival, probably two months or more. The first surviving letter is probably late summer 1917 and is sent from a camp in Scotland[5] (of which more later):

> Dear Sister Tilly
>
> I received your very welcome letter today and was pleased to receive so much news. The chief reason why I have not written before is because I have found it very difficult mentally to be able to clearly state particulars of my experiences.

It is more than likely that he was suffering from confusion and depression from the solitary confinement:

> Firstly I was as you know quite anxious to enter Scrubs, and for the first few days I was fairly contented and as far as I was concerned it was all through but no one only those who have experienced it can say how it really is however much you are prepared there are many shocks as it is a rotten system of treatment everything is given as a punishment and when you have been in a small cell a few days on end it throws you upon your imagination and memories if you have left happiness behind you notice the difference very much and I believe it is more difficult for a C.O. in prison because he does not entertain revenge the same as it generally does an ordinary prisoner which I can well understand.
>
> Unfortunately I was given very hard work being called a cleaner and scrubbing with cold water and no soap for days on end is anything but pleasant, but still this did not affect my acceptance of the HO scheme. Really I am just in the same position now as before I went in I cannot yet decide which is right it was brought home to me that I did not ask absolute exemption it was inconsistent to ask for it or to fight for it in prison.

The conditions and lack of information led to continuous uncertainty of what will happen to him or what choices he might have actually or morally.

> Also I could not parallel work in prison and work outside I think I should

have refused work if I intended to take that position [not clear what he means]. The experiences in prison I would rather tell you than write just now and look forward to seeing you all and tell you about them [was he expecting a visit?]. It has been a great one and also a privilege but it is a great test. The coming out is much worse than the going in. In fact you daren't think of it too much. It is easy to keep awake at night although tired you get funny dreams I can assure you and the opportunity of talking seems almost impossible. You are watched through a small hole by an officer or officers who creep round in canvas shoes. You will no doubt know that some 70 were turned down by the central Tribunal and you will understand that one of the tenterhooks as you never know in prison what is going to happen to you or what news they are going to give you.'[6]

In later life, when interviewed, he was quite mild in his assessment of prison life. When asked about prison food he replied:

No you couldn't get vegetarian meals. There was an attempt, there was an attempt [sic] when I was in Wormwood Scrubs. As a matter of fact the man said he would do without food for a time if they could find him up vegetarian food, see, and apparently they did. They did what they could for him which was rather interesting because to me that was a tremendous thing that there was somebody in prison who was prepared to go without food in prison[,] to go without food for a time because of a principle. That was a marvellous thing I think not many men could do that is there, not many people could do that. I did have a letter about that, come from London. About some people who knew the man who did it. But I never in contact with the man who did it, not since who that happened to. I don't whether he's alive today but there you are.[7]

In retrospect and the passage of time he was very forgiving about the circumstances:

The prison meals had been worked out to a large extent and the amount of food that you were given was almost scientifically arranged out so that you would have sufficient so that you were not suffering from starvation. On the whole the attention given, the official attention given to you with regards to food, personally I wouldn't object to, I couldn't say very much about, because of the conditions, being in wartime. It was a question of how they get the bread made and all sorts of things. Oh no. So consequently I couldn't raise any objections myself.[8]

But at the time, as his letter (2) later reveals, the prisoners were in fact half-starved. He recalled that prisoners wore their own clothes and because it was early summer he found the bedclothes sufficient but the only contact with other prisoners was if a religious service took place and these were controlled by the military. However, although he did not suffer from beatings, the punishments were very harsh and, even in this later recollection he notes the effects of the isolation:

If you're a, that is if you're susceptible person, I mean if you are a person of feeling the punishment can be tremendously hard on you. Say for instance that you're locked up for so long a time and so on all by yourself. I mean, that's a terrible thing As a matter of fact if you've never had that kind of experience you can't imagine what that can be like It can be an awful thing.

Mind you there was just one thing about it that was rather interesting and that is this. In each cell, in each cell, in Wormwood Scrubs there was a Bible. So if a man got a punishment and the rest of it he had the opportunity to read the Bible. He could really look at the Bible. And if he was a CO he could really look at the Bible to support his position.

That's a funny thing having a Bible.[9]

A contemporary writer, Mrs Henry Hobhouse, described the conditions in more detail in her book, *I Appeal Unto Caesar*:

The first twenty-eight days were solitary confinement seeing no one but the warder and occasionally the chaplain. There was no exercise which resulted in headaches and constipation. For the first fourteen days there is no mattress unless the medical officer orders otherwise. After this association with others was allowed although in practice it amount to no more than two hours daily, including exercise and chapel. All conversation throughout the duration of the sentence is forbidden. No prisoner could **write or receive letters until two months into his sentence** and then he can only write and receive one letter and receive one visit from three relatives or friends; the visit last no more than thirty minutes and conducted in the presence of a warder with a thick grille between the prisoner and his visitors. If no visit is possible he may receive and write an additional letter. After this the interval may gradually be reduced to one month if the prisoners conduct is good but in reality the COs did not benefit from this as they were forever being re-sentenced and starting again.

They were not allowed paper or pencil, or any books but the Bible, or news of outside affairs. and relied on a summary of the news given by the Anglican chaplain on Sunday.

...

Punishments are effected through removal of mattresses and diet—Diet 1 is bread and water for up to 15 days, Diet 2 is bread porridge peas and gruel for up to 42 days (6 weeks).

...

Work was scrubbing floors, sewing mail bags or making mattresses but at weekends when no work was done, there was no light given either from 3.30pm on Saturday afternoon until 6 am Sunday.

The sanitary arrangements were also very primitive ...Lack of laundry or change of underclothes, lack of lavatory paper, lack of opportunity to visit the latrine, and only by rote, thus being forced to relieve themselves in their cells. No toothbrushes. Accounts from prisoners includes limited laundry for underwear or towels, change of sheets only every three weeks, no nightwear so sleeping in their clothes. They might get a cold bath once a week, or a warm bath and be sent out into the cold yards and catch chills and fever.

The conditions were made worse by understaffing—the warders having been taken for the war, and by shortage and poverty of food supplies. The prison doctors were often completely unsympathetic.

Men's health broke down or they were extremely physically weakened. Their body functions became irregular, they developed skin diseases, hysteria. They couldn't sleep, their minds went into overdrive of worry about their families or the situation or into torpor, they were mostly very cold and spent their time pacing their stone-floored cells to keep their circulation going, or in some few cases they were over heated by malfunctioning heating pipes with no ventilation. They had very little light and even when later in their sentence they were eventually allowed some reading material it was often very limited or the books were damaged and missing pages.' Some of the countrymen couldn't read and found the isolation even more insupportable, and they became maddened from the isolation.

As a result many took the option of the Home Office Scheme with only about 1,000 choosing to remain in prison.[10]

There is no doubt that conditions were meant to be harsh so that no one should think that conscientious objection was an easy path out of the army. But, as one can see, there was also a sadistic, inhumane streak in the arrangements. What exacerbated the situation was that during Walter's time at Wormwood Scrubs London itself was being bombed by the Germans.

… that prison was completely under fire most of the time I was there you know when the Germans were sending their planes over…..my experience was that when I was there, there were some of the biggest attacks on London that there were at that time when I was there. I believe as a matter of fact, I believe that was the reason why it gave me some deafness. The tremendous effect tremendous noise the bombs made. I think they had some effect upon my nerve centre.[11]

While all Londoners were subjected to these attacks, the prisoners had no way of knowing what was happening or of seeking safety. They were completely at the mercy of circumstances.

> Oh well, as a matter of fact, that's difficult to describe that. You couldn't do anything about it because you were locked in, you see. And you couldn't do anything about it.[12]

In a letter he wrote to a vicar or minister in 1961, Walter recalled one of the most moving experiences he had in Wormwood Scrubs and it illustrates the tone and atmosphere of the incarceration of COs. One night when the prison was 'deathly silent' after a bombing raid Richard Ashley[13], who had been a church vocalist, began singing a hymn and his voice carried through the thick walls and heavy doors. It was a voice in the wilderness bringing hope and for Walter it was an experience of such deep emotion and inspiration that he would never forget it. Prison warders too heard the song and rushed to arrest Ashley and confine him in isolation with bread and water for three days.[14]

It was during his months at Wormwood Scrubs that Walter was at last called before the Central Tribunal.

> Ref. W 3142
> Central Tribunal
> 16 Queen Anne's Gate
> Westminster S.W.1
> 29 March 1917
>
> Sir,
>
> I am desired by the Central Tribunal to inform you that your case has been sent to them by the Army Council in order that the Tribunal may determine, in the light of the information which may now be available, whether you have a conscientious objection to military service based on religious or moral grounds.
>
> Members of the Central Tribunal will attend at Wormwood Scrubs Prison at an early date, when an opportunity will be given to you of being heard by them as to your conscientious objection.
>
> If you do not avail yourself of the opportunity of being heard or if, after having being heard, the Central Tribunal are not satisfied that you have a conscientious objection to military service based on religious or moral grounds, the Central Tribunal are informed that after the completion of your sentence you will be returned to the control of the military authorities.
>
> If, on the other hand, after consideration of your case the Tribunal are satisfied that you have a conscientious objection to military service based on religious or moral grounds. Your case will be sent to the civil

Committee which has been appointed by the Home Office, in order that you may be placed on civil work under civil control and under conditions to be determined by that Committee, and when you take up work you will be transferred to Section W. of the Army Reserve, whereupon you will cease to be subject to military discipline and the Army Act, as also to draw pay from Army funds. You will be allowed to continue at civil work as long as your conduct is satisfactory to the Committee. If you should fail to comply with the conditions laid down by the Committee, you will be sent back to prison to undergo the remainder of your sentence and at the termination of the sentence you will be recalled to Section W. of the Army Reserve and returned to your unit when you will again be fully subject to military discipline and the Army Act.'

Yours faithfully
G Reading
For Central Tribunal
Private Walter Manthorpe[15]

He had at last been officially accepted as a conscientious objector and the next stage was to see what options he had for the future. Absolutists refused all compromise and spent the war in prison under conditions of hard labour. Alternativists accepted alternative service agriculture, forestry, mining, education, food supply and so on.[16] In old age he recalled that:

I stayed in Wormwood Scrubs about two or three months. The reason why I left there was because there was such alarm about the damage that might be done to the prison itself and the risk there was for the prisoners. That was the reason I was sent to Dartmoor - you see - well the chief reason, I think.. Because in Dartmoor Prison they were dealing with COs definitely there although they weren't in Wormwood Scrubs because there were other prisoners besides COs there.[17]

In fact, although it is true that Dartmoor was being prepared to receive COs, it seems that he had accepted the Home Office Scheme as an alternative to staying in prison for the next five years. According to the Peace Pledge Union Website, Walter was listed as an Alternativist and it was on that basis that he was sent to various work camps.[18]

Copy of Undertaking which has been signed by Walter Manthorpe

I, Walter Manthorpe promise for as long as I am allowed to be free from military control and duties:

1. To serve the Committee[19] for the employment of Conscientious Objectors (Hereinafter called the Committee), their Agents and Representatives, with diligence and fidelity on such work of National Importance as the Committee may prescribe for me.

2. To reside at such place as the Committee, their Agents or Representatives, may from time to time determine.
3. To conform to such regulations as the Committee may lay down for the due execution of the work allotted to me.
4. To conform to such regulations with regard to conduct and to such as are farmed to secure the well-being of men working under similar conditions to myself as may be made by the Committee or by the Agents or the Representatives of the Committee or as may be made by duly appointed Representatives of the men working and approved by the Committee.

I understand that these are the conditions on which I am released and if and when I cease to carry out any of the foregoing conditions I shall be liable to complete the term of my sentence and subsequently to be recalled to military service.

(Signed) W. Manthorpe

According to the Peace Pledge Union, the Home Office Scheme 'entailed agreeing to perform civilian work under civilian control in specially created Work Centres/Work Camps. Refusal to accept the Scheme meant returning to prison to complete the sentence, then returning to the Army, where renewed disobedience would entail another court-martial and another prison sentence.'

The Work Centres were all over the country and COs were sent as far away from home as possible:

Ballachulish, Scotland
Brockenhurst, Hants
Broxburn, Lothian, Scotland
Denton, Newhaven, Sussex
Derry, Ormond
Ditton Priors, Shropshire
Dyce, Aberdeen
Knutsford, Cheshire (Knutsford Prison)
Llanddeusant, Wales
Longside, Aberdeenshire
Minworth, Warwicks
Penderyn, Wales
Princetown, Devon (Dartmoor Prison)
Red Roses, Whitland, Carmarthen
Risbridge House, Kedington, Suffolk
Sandholme Brick & Tile Works, Sandholme, East Riding, Yorks.
Sunk Island, Hull
Sutton, Surrey

Talgarth, Wales
Uphall, West Lothian
Wakefield, Yorkshire (Wakefield Prison)
Warwick, Warwickshire (Warwick Prison)

The British Army's increasing need for troops was generally framed to the public in terms of sacrifice, an idea that would be easily understandable in a Christian culture: sacrifice for country, for family, for friends; sacrifice for ultimate victory and peace. John Rae in his *Conscience and Politics*, argues that public opinion demanded from COs 'a sacrifice that was comparable if not identical to that made by the soldiers.'[20] Indeed, the peace movement itself used this imagery and was not slow to publicise the deprivations of its members.[21] By June 1917, members of the Norwich Society of Friends were urging the Meeting to take action in the Peace Cause.

Despite the Home Office Scheme describing the paid-but-compulsory work for non-combatants as of national importance, in fact it was generally pointless, back breaking and rough. The temporary camps and converted prisons were run by civilian warders but the men were liable to be returned to prison for any 'trivial irregularity.'[22] Although, to a great degree, the men supervised themselves and formed committees for various purposes this was within enforced restrictions and subject to stringent punishments. *'Not only is the work futile, but the conditions under which it is performed are those most calculated to discourage the worker'*[23] The physical conditions and the work demanded were extreme and punitive, the food was meagre and access to medical treatment sems to have been very limited and administered by the medical profession with ill-will.

Some COs were highly trained and their skills could have been employed productively but they were not. Even market gardeners, whose lands went to waste just when produce was most needed, were not utilised. The government had no interest in harnessing their various capabilities for 'work of national importance'. With rising casualties at the Front, public opinion about COs had soured into resentment and distrust and there was criticism of the laxity of the camps especially where the men had access to the local population after working hours. The punitive conditions were created to deter conscientious objection and to placate boorish public opinion fanned by the Harmsworth press.[24] The last thing the government needed was for the public to question the authority of the military or legislative hierarchy or their effectiveness.

By and large, the religious COs—the Quakers, Tolstoians, Methodists, Plymouth Brethren—and the intellectuals, were co-operative and kept to the regulations. They were patriotic as long as they didn't have to fight, although the more religiously fanatical could be bothersome in their zealous enthusiasm. But with the political objectors it was another matter. The communists, anarchists and ILP members often had no respect for the government and were only too happy to cause trouble and try to promote their own causes. They were not by definition anti-violence and, given the chance, some would not only try to escape but probably have cheerfully taken up arms against capitalism.

Notes

1. Letter 2, from Scotland summer of 1917.
2. Burnham, K. *The Courage of Cowards*, 2014, p. 70.
3. Goodall, F. *We Will Not Go to War: Conscientious Objection During The World Wars*, 2013, p. 41. When he was transferred to Lincoln Prison it was the Sinn Fein prisoners who helped him survive.
4. Letter to an unknown correspondent, a church minister, 15 November, 1961—a copy survives.
5. Letter 2. Road Board Camp, Caolasnacon, Ballachulish, Scotland. Dated only 'Wednesday' summer 1917.
6. Ibid.
7. Reel 5, IWM tapes.
8. Ibid.
9. Ibid.
10. Hobhouse, H. *I Appeal Unto Caesar : The Case Of The Conscientious Objector*, 1918, p. 45.
11. Reel 4, IWM tapes.
12. Ibid.
13. Richard Ashley, one of four CO brothers from 120 Churchill Road, Norwich. Richard Ashley was a member of the Independent Labour Party as well as the No-Conscription Fellowship, he died not long after World War I probably as a result of his treatment. It was his brother Jack Ashley who became Walter's close friend.
14. Letter to an unknown correspondent November 15, 1961.
15. Document in the possession of the author.
16. Bouton, David. *Objection Overruled*, 1967, p. 132.
17. Reel 4, IWM tapes.
18. https://menwhosaidno.org/men/men_files/m/manthorpe_walter_frederic.html, accessed 23/03/2021.
19. The Brace Committee, presumably.
20. Rae, John. *Conscience and Politics*, 1970, p. 169.
21. Bibbings, pp. 152-4.
22. Graham, John William. *Conscription and Conscience: A History, 1916-1919*, 1922, p. 244.
23. Ibid, p. 236.
24. Ibid, p. 237. 'Newspapermen were sent down to Princeton for the purpose of taking pictures and seeking interviews. They were admitted by the authorities. Idleness and self-indulgence were freely ascribed to these worried and suffering men.' The result was storms of questions in Parliament and indignant local meetings in Plymouth.

21. Entrance to Dartmoor Prison.

4. Spring/Summer 1917–Autumn 1917

After three months in Wormwood Scrubs, in the early summer of 1917 Walter made the journey to Dartmoor now renamed Princeton Work Camp.

His autumn 1917 letter to his sister Tilly recounts:

> When I came out I was very weak as they reduced rations before I left they sent us off to Princetown in a snowstorm with no arrangements on the journey and you can perhaps imagine how I felt. In Scrubbs I met many men and could write volumes about the little ways I found out also the dodges. If you can imagine a chap eating his beeswax which he used in his work and a chap you know ate a tallow (piece) he was so hungry.[1]

At Princetown, about six hundred men were housed in the recently evacuated prison that came with about 2,000 acres of land. About fifty were employed in land reclamation for the Duchy of Cornwall.

The agricultural work was designed to be as tiring as possible. In a letter to the *Manchester Guardian* a woman called Lydia Smith testified to having seen a gang of eight men harnessed to a roller engaged in rolling a field that one man and a horse could have accomplished in half the time. Weeks were spent digging fields by hand that could have been ploughed by machine. She notes that these men had calculated that each turnip grown (for livestock), would have cost the government ninepence, which also shows that the COs were not stupid and their brains could have been put to better use.

> The spades, barrows, etc are all prodigiously heavy, with a view to tiring the users, and all the appliances and methods are of the most antiquated nature.'[2] 'Applications for improved tools were consistently refused by the Home Office and despite there being many horses on the farm, the men were forced to do everything by hand.[3]

Much of the work involved quarrying—stone breaking—carpentry, blacksmithing and prison industries. The hours were exceptionally long, breaks very few. The scheme was penal in all but name and the conditions were worse and the pay of eight pence a day, which was two-thirds of the minimum pay of a private in the army, was less than for criminals.

This was a turbulent time in the history of the Home Office Scheme. According to Graham a police spy had been sent into the camp to inveigle COs into breaking the rules and although most COs had not risen to the bait, there had been an

22. Coal party at Dartmoor.

incident involving a cup of milk brought in for a sick CO. Sir C. Kinloch-Cooke, the Unionist MP for Devonport, pursued the issue of COs treatment vindictively and energetically. As a result, from the autumn of 1917 there was more discipline. Leave was cancelled, hours of freedom reduced, amounts of food reduced and the wages of men with families.[4]

This was not a good time to have arrived but, for better or worse, Walter was only at Princeton a short time before, at some point in April, he was sent up to west Scotland to another work camp at Caolasnacon and it is from here that his next surviving undated (possibly April/May) letter originates.[5] He had travelled by train on a fifty-hour journey - two days and two nights - that almost certainly had no facilities of any sort. After that they crossed Loch Leven in a boat:

He wrote to his sister:

> This Camp is well arranged and fitted up the work is hard roadmaking in fact it is a lovely spot you have perhaps found it on the map.[6]

Walter immediately met up with Donald Ashley, one of the four Ashley brothers from Norwich, and received some welcome news from him. He had also received a copy of *The Tribunal*[7] from Tilly[8] and found out much about the COs situation which he said would have been helpful to him had he known earlier. Presumably

23. Contemporary view of the village of Princeton and the Work Camp.

this would have influenced his limited choices with regard to the Home Office Scheme.

> There are men here (200) from all parts and all different opinions. There is some discussion. There are 80 vegetarians including myself and we exchange opinion during work it is very laughable [he may mean ironic or amusing]. We are in huts 30 in each and are 3 miles from any houses being on the side of Loch Leven, between Ballachulish and Kinlockleven, and near the scene of the battle of Glencoe or rather massacre.
>
> …
>
> Shortly I shall be forwarding on some postcards but don't wait for them if you have any news or questions to ask all news is acceptable my time is pretty much taken up as I have such a lot of writing to do but hope you will at any rate have an idea of my doings
>
> Believe me
> I remain
> Your affectionate brother
> xxxxxx
>
> I send these [kisses] but of course the Manthorpe family rarely make use of them.⁹

The work was stone breaking in the quarry for road construction. The sister camp at Dyce already had a bad reputation since the English COs, most of whom were

24. The COs Landing Stage at Loch Leven.
The nearest village was 4 miles away. Walter was here from April to June 1917.

well-educated and articulate, had been housed in old Boer War tents that leaked and this resulted in poor health and one death in September 1916. The *Aberdeen Daily Journal* called them 'shirkers' and 'degenerates'. That camp was closed and the Caolasnacon camp now had wooden huts.

25. The wooden huts which formed the work camp at Caolasnacon.

He wrote to Tilly on 13 June, 1917:

> Dear Sister Tilly
>
> Was very pleased to receive your welcome letter today and hasten to answer it. You say that you forwarded me one a fortnight ago which was quite right as I received it and did not answer which I hope you will forgive especially as it was so interesting…What has happened these last few weeks has been that I have written about 3 letters per day having had a lot of writing to do which I am glad of being so pleased at hearing how everything is going on.[10]

It is not clear whether all these letters are personal or to do with the work of the Friends and the Non-Conscription Fellowship, or to his trying to find work, as he goes on to explain:

> At present I am trying to find a solution to several problems [most probably health problems] (you know this is a weakness of mine). I am not satisfied in letting circumstances affecting me more than I can help. I am ambitious enough to believe that I can do better than I am at present even if it means prison again. (don't tell Ma and Pa this). The Friends Service Comm. have offered me work and I am still in communication with them. [It is unclear what this means as he stayed in the Work Camp scheme] What I want is to feel that I am doing something coinciding with what I believe to be a conscientious attitude.[11]

This inner strength, the discipline of mind, which he was able to utilise in this

26. *Group of COs at Caolasnacon Camp, in front of a hut labelled 'The Jawbox' by Walter, who wrote the sign, is standing in the back row, fourth from right.*

difficult time had been cultivated by Quaker practice of silent communion within the weekly meetings for worship.

> It is pleasing news about Father I know there must be difficult times from both Ma and Pa it is not easy for them to stand the strain. At one time I used to believe in worrying but now I have come to the conclusion it is a sin. I was pleased to read your remarks about yourself I hope I will maintain this attitude. I only wish we as a family had been more ambitious and I wish you every success. As to myself my health is improving but I just find that many things I was conversant of before going to prison are difficult to bring to memory yet. This will take time to remedy and will come eventually.

This loss of memory was most likely due to the effects of solitary confinement, the effects of which were known, even at the time, and especially amongst the absolutists.[12] Since psychologists have begun studying it, solitary confinement is now recognised as a form of torture; the symptoms can include anxiety, panic, insomnia, digestive problems and post-traumatic stress disorder. It has recently been argued that periods of isolation, even less than ten days, can have long-term effects, with the presence—up to three years later—of psychiatric symptoms.[13] But notice again Walter's positivity: he felt sure that the effects will wear off in time. His letter returned to external events and his hopes for the future:

> Your news about the Leeds conference[14] I have distributed here and it was welcomed. It is to be noted that advancement is being made I certainly think that the silver lining is in sight, and we must look forward with hope to a measure of returned liberty.[15]

The Leeds convention established a Council of Workers' and Soldiers' Delegates and was inspired by the Russian February 1917 Revolution. It was organised by the United Socialist Council and speakers included Ramsay Macdonald, Bertrand Russell and Sylvia Pankhurst. It called for an end to the war and the restoration of civil liberties, including the release of conscientious objectors. It evidently raised hopes amongst COs of a political breakthrough but the Bolshevik October Revolution prompted the collapse of the Council.

> We have no definite notice of leaving here yet and although many rumours are afloat no doubt something definite will turn up shortly. It is difficult to explain to Ma and Pa in a letter about my position here and the attitude I have taken. I feel very much about the mistaken attitude of many of the patriotic sacrifices of many we know but how tragically mistaken. We have all had some percentage of choice heaven only knows how difficult mine was I could not and you cannot tell what it meant to me. I only hope I have contributed a small part toward a hope of liberty for the future. You can well see how liberty and opportunity have absolutely been stifled by the so-called powers that be. You can depend upon the fact that many contests

will have to be faced for liberty to be the right of the people. There is much I have to tell and I hope it will not be so long before I shall be able to be nearer to you than I am at present to discuss these things with you.[16]

This letter is one of the clearest with regard to Walter's attitude to conscientious objection. It is not simply a matter of religious conviction regarding killing, it is about a whole social and political system that represses common people and dictates how they will live their lives. It's about liberty itself. What is interesting is that his ideas about liberty of the individual seem to have expanded, presumably through the extensive conversations amongst the COs. The effect of putting all these men together was that they honed their ideas through debate and exchange of experience.

It's unclear how long he was in Scotland, some weeks or a few months. Long enough to recover both some health and his spirit, and to have one adventure which he revealed years later in his Imperial War Museum interview:

> We got the freedom on the Sunday. [time off] You see. And that's how we did it. The hours of work finished up on the Saturday and soon as we finished up we walked off to Ben Nevis and walked northward. We couldn't go by train. I think that's too complicated to take up on this one.

27. Walter kept this photograph folded in his wallet and it looks to be of a group of COs in a landscape of ferns and rocks that could well be the climbing expedition to Ben Nevis.

We stayed at a house at night time - a woman put us up in bed at night time near Ben Nevis and we climbed it on the Sunday and come down and got back on the Sunday night.[17]

It seems extraordinary under their very constrained circumstances that the group thought of climbing Ben Nevis and then undertook the expedition. It seems, as much as anything, to signal their determination to maintain some autonomy in their lives.

At some point in the autumn the Caolasnacon camp was closed and the COs sent south to Wakefield prison near Leeds, a very old prison, notorious for its unsavoury criminals, which had been made over into a Home Office Camp.[18] Living conditions here were better than in Scotland but the penal work continued. In *Conscription and Conflict*, John William Graham describes it:

> The prison at Wakefield had been transformed; the locks had been taken from the doors of the cells; dining tables were placed in the broad corridors, and the warders—out of uniform—acted as instructors. The doctor acted as the head of the establishment. The work was the usual prison work: mailbags, mats etc. Work stopped at five in the afternoon, and the six hundred men could spend their evening in or out until 9.30. The Friends' Meeting House was again turned into a social centre, and men were frequently welcomed at the meeting houses at Bradford and at Leeds. For a long time the efforts of the hostile local Press did not produce any hostility among the townspeople; later on a gang of roughs was organized to attack the COs as they returned to the prison in the evenings.[19]

Nevertheless discontent was rife largely because of the changes in the Home Office Scheme rules which now denied the prisoners any leave to go home and reduced their wages. He wrote to his sister a week after his arrival:

> As you know we are in the prison premises and which let me say couldn't be improved upon for such a purpose as this. There is every convenience and I expect it has been very interesting to the COs relatives who have had a look round. My particular work is making special mail bags which we do out in the open air which is alright all the boys work inside the prison in different shops. There are several Norwich boys. One named Watering, Wise and Jack and Lewes Ashley, these both having just arrived. At present a Questionnaire is being conducted where we are all asked about our position in regard to the scheme and as far as I can make out they want to get an idea how many would be willing to repudiate the Scheme. Your remarks about obeying rules is rather a burning question here. What is stated which is quite true is that the conditions made when we accepted the Scheme have been entirely altered. They have taken leave away and altered many other things. This is no doubt mostly our own faults let it

28. Wakefield Prison cells.   29. Cell at Wakefield Prison.

be said. Personally I am not one these repudiators but the movement is anything but small and many things might happen.[20]

Walter was able to take advantage of the urban location and the comparative freedom:

> Yesterday I had a train ride to look at Leeds there was some crowds and it was very interesting. Our presence goes unnoticed and I have not heard one remark antagonistic up to the present. The food here is very decent. I am still a veg.[vegetarian] And I feel quite satisfied with it, it agrees with me. Your remarks in one of your letters about the difference between us and the soldiers in France came forcibly to me when talking to a Canadian soldier in Leeds. He said he joined up because he did not want to be forced to join although he might have been a C.O. he did not know what we were and we did not tell him. Don't you think every soldier has a choice no doubt circumstances had a lot to do with the majority but if I told you of cases of men here and their circumstances you would perhaps think as I do that it is difficult to compare us because we all had to chose [sic] more or less what we should do.[21]

30. Exercise rings at Wakefield Prison.

According to his interview in 1974 no members of the family ever visited him. It's possible that he had forgotten but if they did not, I imagine it would have been because it was beyond their financial capability and also they were all working. They did however, regularly send food parcels which accounted for his survival in anything like reasonable health.

Walter was not in Wakefield for long. He was sent for more hard labour to a camp at Talgarth on the edge of the Brecon Beacons, Wales which was opened in July 1917. Wales had a more extreme experience of the Great War than England. On the one hand the long tradition of non-conformity tolerated or supported conscientious objection, on the other there were localised currents of deep prejudice against people of German origin once the war began. Ideas of Welsh nationalism were beginning to emerge which also created a tension in fighting a war for the English. Low church rigid morality condemned women who consorted with soldiers while female employment was very low and poorly paid. Generally, the war hit Wales very hard in economic terms.[22]

The work at Talgarth was digging trenches for drainage and water supplies for a new sanatorium erected by the Welsh National memorial association.[23] 'This tough work meant working ten hours per day in two five-hour shifts and the food was considered to be 'quite inadequate' for the nature of the work. The accommodation was also sub-standard: tents, old cottages and barns. This led to considerable discontent and flouting of the rules. It was from Talgarth that Walter wrote his next letter to Tilly but only some undated pages of the letter survive, but must be pre-July because he mentions the Stockholm Conference.

> Most of the men say that the man who works the hardest and fulfils his agreement get sent to the worst jobs and the worst conditions, like manure work [Edinburgh] and stone breaking, where the men are quartered in common lodging houses. As to Austin Ashley I do not agree with his position although I know he has good reason for his actions. I have endeavoured to fulfil my contract and haven't a complaint against me yet. There is no doubt the coming of the Stockholm Conference[24] will show us whether the Leeds meetings[25] were really successful. Personally I am rather impatient about these things but no doubt I have reasons.[26]

It is unclear whether he was impatient for these peace initiatives to succeed or whether he was impatient with the political manoeuvring that were rumbling in the background.

> The other day Jack Ashley who is here with me told me that the Rev Dunnico held a meeting at Goat Lane. You have not mentioned this. I hope it was a good meeting. Tom Archer has not written from Dartmoor. I heard things were improving there and I expect he is still there.[27]

He goes on to describe the effects of the diet and conditions in which they were kept:

> Would you like to come to Wales for your holiday. It's alright for a holiday but hardly the same for work. You ask me about my boils. I have had an epidemic of them round the neck and they have been continuous for a time till this week when I hope I shall have seen the last of them. They have been very painful and the doctor told me they were the result of coarse living. You ask me about the work here. We are doing navvy work and doing drainage work which means digging trenches up to 10 feet deep there is about 2 miles to do and we work 5 hour stretches on insufficient grub barring parcels from home. Don't paint this too black to anybody because I wrote and told you I had boils but hadn't told Jennie [his wife] consequently I got into a row. It is so difficult to know how to sum up the war at present. I do think that things are hopeful and I look forward to having Xmas dinner in Norwich it is quite possible. The people here are quite sympathetic and treat us very decently. Our particular quarters are in Lloyd George Sanitorium which is a large one and is being built, there are no particular comforts. I won't enumerate them because it doesn't do to dwell on troubles. I don't do that if I can help it. You can guess being C.O.s they would be careful as to who they chose as gangers and we have one here, one of the old navvy type. swears and drinks heavily and eats like an elephant but he is in my opinion the best one I have met as he says what he means straight out.[28]

This is borne out by the testimony of another CO, Alfred Evans:

> I was on the Home Office Scheme and I went down to South Wales to work on the waterworks and it was a slave driving job and they put professional slave drivers over us, people who had been slave drivers over African natives.[29]

Alfred Evans called a strike and was sent back to prison as a result.[30] The troublemakers and escapees tended to be socialists or Marxists who had only contempt for the system.[31]

Walter's lengthy letter to Tilly describes the conditions which prompted the strike:

> There has been trouble here with the agent [the Home Office Scheme Agent] ever since we have been here… We were up[un]till Sat allowed 2 A(?) cake on Sat mornings if we worked 6 hours which is up till 1 ocl [o'clock] but this week without notice withdrew it. Our men refuse do work 6 hours in wet trenches without a rest and the agent have kept back the money which we are generally paid. 4/8 single men ½ married.[32] [i.e. 4/8 married men, 2/4 single men]

Apparently the Home Office agent fined two men two weeks' pay on two occasions for ceasing work at twelve o'clock (the usual dinner hour).

> There is heaps to tell you I could write reames of paper but I think I have answered most of your questions and shall look forward to the next consignment. Things are moving fast. Personally I look forward to the future because the past belongs to the past[,] the future is with us. There is room for much hope.
>
> I remain
> Your C.O. brother
> Posh
> xxxxx
> xxxx[33]

Against this backdrop of physical exhaustion and starvation rations, Walter, ever the constructive individual, was attempting not to rebel but to get himself in a better position by applying through the Society of Friends for work outside the Home Office camps. In particular he was looking for work in Birmingham which, through the Cadburys, had a long tradition of prominent Quakers. It was also home to Pitman's vegetarian hotel. His letters to his parents are much simpler and less detailed than those to his sister. They were less educated people but also probably not fully engaged in what was going on, unlike his sister who was dedicated to the cause and playing her part through the Quaker initiatives. His undated letter from the autumn of 1917 thanks his parents for the food supplies they send and also his rather tentative hopes:

San Lodge Box
Talgarth
Breconshire
Wales

Thursday

Dear Ma Pa and all

Was glad to receive your welcome parcel which arrived quite safe and sound without even an egg cracked. Everything was appreciated and you sent just what I wanted. I haven't tested the jam yet but it looks good. There is not much news, we hear that the religious objectors are likely to be sent home. And the Friends wrote to me from London asking what meeting I belonged to so perhaps there is something in it.

It is very cold here now but very healthy. I am feeling quite well. This air seems to suit me. Have not yet had any reply from Birmingham so am wondering what will happen, but will let you know as soon as I am transferred if it comes off. Hope you are all well and received my letter I sent off Sunday last. Please remember me to all who know me, I send best love to all

And remain
Your loving son and brother
Walter.[34]

Notes

1. Letter 2.
2. From a letter by Lydia S. Smith to the *Manchester Guardian*, quoted in Graham, p. 236. n
3. Graham, p. 237.
4. Graham, p. 239.
5. Letter 2 from Road Board Camp, Caolasnacon, Ballachulish.
6. Ibid.
7. *The Tribunal* was the Quaker newsletter for and about COs.
8. The role of Quaker women in supporting the COs and the peace movement seems to be largely undocumented.
9. Letter 2. A sad comment on the lack of emotional demonstration in the family, which Walter, a warm man, evidently regretted..
10. Letter 3, June 13 1917.
11. Ibid.
12. Kramer, Ann. *Conscientious Objectors of the First World War*, 2014, p. 143.
13. *The Lancet* Brooks et al 2020.
14. The Leeds Convention held on 3 June 1917 … saw 3,500 people from across Britain gather at the Leeds Coliseum (now the O2 Academy) in solidarity with the February

Revolution which had overthrown the brutal Tsarist autocracy in Russia. The Convention voted to... call for an end to the First World War and vote to set up Workers' and Soldiers' Councils in Britain in solidarity with the Soviets being formed in revolutionary Russia. *https://legaciesofwar.leeds.ac.uk/events/event-to-mark-the-centenary-of-the-leeds-convention-1917/*

15. Letter 3.
16. Ibid.
17. Reel 4, IWM tapes.
18. His 1970s memories of his movements between camps contradict the dates of letters.
19. Graham, p. 233.
20. Letter 4.
21. Ibid.
22. Hulonce, Lesley. Pulpits, mutinies and 'khaki fever'; *World War One in Wales. https://ahrc.ukri.org/research/fundedthemesandprogrammes/worldwaroneanditslegacy/world-war-one-at-home/ww1inwales/pulpitsmutinieskhakifever/*
23. Referred to in the PhD thesis of Aled Eirug, 'Opposition the First World War in Wales', Cardiff University, 2016.
24. July and August 1917 a socialist conference to determine how best to encourage international workers' solidarity in pursuit of peace. Many countries banned the attendance of delegates and the Conference was ineffectual.
25. A Labour and Socialist Convention held in June 1917 to discuss the implications of the first Russian Revolution.
26. Letter 5.
27. Ibid. Thomas James Walter Archer from 4, Bulman's Nursery, Northgate Street, Great Yarmouth.
28. Ibid.
29. Quoted in Goodhall, 2013, p. 58. A rather shocking reflection on colonial practices.
30. Ibid.
31. Aled Eirug points out that 'Even after the end of the war, the authorities pursued recalcitrant objectors.', p. 244.
32. An NCF news sheet for the Home Office Centres and Camps, Acc 13388, Autumn 1917, National Library of Scotland, quoted by Aled Eirug, bears this out.
33. Letter 5.
34. Letter 8.

5. September 1917–February 1918

At the beginning of September 1917 Walter wrote again to his sister Tilly to give her a broader picture of his circumstances in Wales. Evidently there was sympathy from local people with the COs and Walter was still optimistic about a political initiative for peace from international workers:

> Although as you say our job takes some sticking we are I think the happier crowd today, no widows or orphans will mark our path and it is because of these things we have a certain amount of contentment. The other day I took our laundry to a farmhouse where the woman told me she had two sons at the War. She remarked that she wished they had been a bit longer headed as she found we had been. It has on the surface been a bit disappointing about Stockholm, but apparently to me the delay is for the best: the more united and strong the peace forces become the more far reaching the consequences, and it is coming. It was interesting to read about the repudiation of G Roberts[1] there will be more heard about his case by the L Leader of the week. The news about Mr Libby Read I was sorry to hear about as I saw him at Britannia Barracks when I was there, hope to hear better news of him.[2] I expect this letter will reach you on holiday and hope you are having a good time you lucky beggars, please remember me to all you meet who know me.[3]

This asking to be remembered to his friends is a recurring theme and indicates the isolation and ostracism he was feeling. But he returns again to the political themes of the position of the citizen with regard to the state:

> There are numbers of things going on in this England which seems impossible and how men are being treated. If you do get a chance do all you can to forward opportunities as to releasing the absolutists, I believe resolutions are being sent, all of us here are practically unanimous that they should be unconditionally released and I am sure if you only knew what they are sticking you would with me be stirred with indignation at their treatment.[4]

Now, also, he was more forthright about the treatment the COs had received and it becomes clear that he himself was systematically starved at Wormwood Scrubs.

> Today I have seen a letter signed by three men who are again being court martialled who say they are being systematically tortured by being gradually starved and knowing what this means I feel very strongly about it.[5]

He then returned to comment on life in Norwich and the price of groceries—

his old boss Mr Eddington was evidently doing well out of the war prices and shortages.

> By your letter Mr E [Alexander Eddington] is still leading the van in prices no wonder he has made good profits. You might tell mother for her benefit that my boils have all disappeared and I feel more comfortable here than anywhere I have been yet. It isn't all clover but the air here suits me and there are some nice people about here who are quite friendly. She might have something to worry about if there was more of a chance of me coming home with an arm or a leg missing or not at all. Although the last part of the sentence ought to be omitted because comparisons like these do not ought to be introduced. When I took the position I did I had to be prepared to accept everything that came along and content myself that things could be worse.[6]
>
> [no more]

A month later he wrote again to Tilly from Wales and was still hoping he may be released by Christmas. She had sent news of Percy J. Boddy.

> Oct 4 1917
>
> Dear Sister Tilly
>
> And all, was very glad to receive your letter and also to hear you were getting somewhat used to your new furniture, I should like to have a look at you. Let's hope we shall celebrate an Xmas without a War but its not certain yet as the blockheads are still ruling things, still we are hopeful that something will turn up shortly. Sorry to hear Percy[7] has received calling up papers let's hope he won't pay too dear for his experience, he will find prison a decent test. May he get through with fortitude. He has my best wishes. If you hear about W Newby let me know as I should like to know how he is getting on I often think about him.[8] It's quite right about Mary[9], she has done splendidly and Norwich N.C.F. would be much poorer without her.[10] Of course being absent from home we count very much on receiving letters. I saw the report of the death of T Bryan[11] what a loss he is and what a man. As you say the H.F.S.[12] goes on alright, it has proved its existence and it may see the War through.[13]

It seems that his knowledge of food led to him being appointed Canteen Manager for the camp and his efforts to get himself employed outside the Home Office Scheme continued:

> Sunday night
>
> Since I began the letter I have been busy with one thing and another. I

am canteen manager here and have a fairly busy time. This week I have had a good offer from Pitmans of Birmingham[14] who would like to get me transferred there. The agent here has written the Home Office on the matter but I am not certain of the job coming off although it would be splendid if it did.

Then surprisingly he reveals that the local Welsh women have taken a shine to the COs in their midst:

> You ask me in your letter whether I have made many friends, what happens is this at present that I have just made friends with the Grocer in the town and have been at his house he has a shop a café, and a Hotel besides 3 or 4 cars. They are nice people and I get on alright with them. They are not conversant with Social question or some of the subjects I have dabbled in so we have some good talks It is a treat to get in one of their comfortable armchairs near a fire as a change to the camp. What is remarkable here is the blooming girls. They won't leave me alone their special walks bring them near the camp and whenever you go out as there is only one road to Talgarth you can't miss them. It's a good job I am married they seem to have a good opinion of us and there are crowds of them. A remarkable case is of two maids who are at this Sanitorium both of whom have lost their fathers in the war. They told one of our fellows that although this has happened they would rather this has happened because they think their experiences in France would not have been beneficial should they have returned, and neither will be friendly with soldiers.[15]

This is a sharp contrast to the propaganda of the day which suggested that COs were unmanly and unattractive to women. It's also interesting that the women are already thinking about the poor mental condition or trauma of returning soldiers. Problems of maintaining adequate living conditions continue:

> After some agitation we have got a common room with a stove in where fellows can read and write letters in and also have meetings and this is the only kind of warmth the men have in the quarters which are a good distance from the Cook House. Most of the men are working some 2 miles away from here now they are getting on fairly well with the work.

The Home Office Scheme continued to be unsatisfactory to nearly all concerned.

> There are all sorts of rumours afloat about the Scheme, either the COs will get broken or the Scheme will[,] the crisis is coming as you have perhaps guessed by remarks made by those in it. Numbers are growing the C.O. Flying Corps, and numbers are repudiating it every week. Most of the camps are in a ferment the restrictions are getting worse and as you perhaps have heard Edwin Gilbert[16] has resigned because of this at Wakefield. Jack Ashley is at present Chairman here and his chum

Rowlands is Sec.[17] It has been a continual fight since we came here and will be as far as I can see. The previous committee and Chairman & sec have nearly all been removed or done a moonlight. There is good reason for thinking something is going to happen shortly as I hear B Russell [Bertrand Russell] of the NCF has stated, we are all going to be given Pelham Committee but no official news has come through, of course I am more than fed up but I intend to stick it as long as I can as I feel an improvement in myself I intend to continue.[18]

'To be given Pelham Committee' meant to be allowed to return to civil employment in some way or another. Walter is still hopeful but knows that his strength is much reliant on the food parcels being sent from home:

I'm afraid if it wasn't for help from home in the way of grub I should feel different to what I do as things are not up to much without this. Last week I read the book just out called "I Appeal Unto Caesar" which you have perhaps read. It states the position of the C.O. well and will help to do which I am certain will happen and that is the education of the public to our position and also as to the War. The tide is turning and soon the flood of revulsion to the so-called altruistic morals of the Warmongers will be found out. Since I have been on this Scheme I have collected a nice lot of views of one thing and another and I hope <u>one day</u> to be able to show you them I must have 2 xxx [days?] I should think. The most interesting I think though will be the episodes that pen and paper are unable to reproduce, they are carefully stored away for future use.[19] This is all I can think of at the moment and hoping this will find you well as I am also Ma, Pa and Annie

I remain
Your loving brother
Walter.[20]

He had been trying to garner support, and opportunities for work. It is evident that even those who supported COs were now seeing and hearing such terrible reports from the Front, that their sympathies were hard stretched as this letter from Herbert Day:

Woodhurst [82 Newmarket Road]
Norwich

Dear Manthorpe

I was glad to hear from you, as though I have tried, I have been unable to find work for you. There is no doubt there is feeling against C.O.s and although unjust we can understand it. This morning I hear from a great friend, who has 3 sons out in France, one has lost his leg, one he has just heard is killed and the third is still there.

You are safe from all that, by the law of the land. So try and do whatever you are asked to do willingly. I know it is hard and disagreeable but we are all Englishmen, and obtain great privileges in many ways. So though we do not believe in fighting and killing anyone in these times short of that we should be ready to do what we are asked.

Why you are asked to do disagreeable duties, is no doubt because others feel that a C.O. should not be much better off than those who are going through the awful existence at the Front. Do not feel that you are a criminal but that you are sharing a terrible experience with your fellow countrymen and in many ways not so terrible as theirs, with best wishes and kind regards

Sincerely yours

Herbert A. Day.[21]

Then something happened that changed Walter's course again. He and another CO were asked to spy on their fellow workers and give information about them to the authorities.

> … a man took me on one side and asked me if I would give private details as to the men that were there and what they were doing and all the rest of it. I couldn't do that. It wasn't fair for me to do that. He turned around and said you'll have to go back to Dartmoor. That was a bit of a scare but anyway that's what they did.[22]

Presumably the authorities wanted information about the men's political activities or any plans they had to rebel against the regulations. Walter was summarily removed from the work camp but they must have thought he was trustworthy because:

> And the funny thing was they give me the ticket or the money to buy the ticket at the station and simply left me to go there by myself. There was nobody sent with me. I had to do that by myself and I did it. Think of that.[23]

In a later letter (20 January 1918) he elaborated the details of his trip from Wales to Dartmoor and including the practical involvement of the NCF in finding them accommodation. It is not quite clear how the expenses allowance worked. He seemed to imply that rather than going from Bristol to Dartmoor direct, they diverted to London.

> I don't know whether I told you what happened when I was coming here from Wales we were two days coming down and had to borrow money in Bristol to stop the night. We found up the Sec of the NCF who made us comfortable and shew us a decent coffee house. It was through an air raid in London that we were detained and after getting here I claimed expenses

from the HO which they allowed us, anyway part of them.[24]

It was early December and he was heading back to Dartmoor. Winter was well underway and Walter headed one of his letters with the Princetown address and added 'Otherwise Siberia' indicating the conditions.

He was assigned to room 37 in Hall 2. The work continued, heavy and unrelenting,

31. Entrance archway to Dartmoor Prison.

and the COs were ill-equipped for the task either physically or in terms of clothing. They worked ten-hour shifts on weekdays and six and a half hours on Saturdays doing utterly pointless work. Later Walter recalled fainting while doing agricultural duties:

> Q. What kind of work did you have to do in prison, was it difficult? Was it useful?
>
> A. Well, at Dartmoor for instance I was sent to dig in the garden. And I did it and I went unconscious. It knocked me completely out. Then after that I was given the job of… of… of dealing with stones, dealing with stones, (sic) stone work. That was very different. It wasn't so heavy work as what the digging was, you see. I could do that. That was very difficult work at Dartmoor, to sort of shape stones…not ordinary stones, but I mean like gravestones, things like that, that was the kind of stones it was. But you had to use the hammer and chisel to do that.[25]

The men were fashioning what were called DCP (Dartmoor Convict Prison)

32. Punishment cells at Dartmoor.

boundstones.

They were also set to road building and today their handywork can be seen in what has been called the 'Road to Nowhere'. More commonly known as the 'Conchies Road' this track made its way in a south easterly direction towards the river Swincombe. The road is clearly visible on an aerial photograph and is still used today by many walkers.[26]

However, there were some advantages to being at Dartmoor one of which was the large numbers of COs—over 1,000—providing the possibility of greater social exchange especially on Sunday when there were a good many religious services available.[27]

There was also a considerable amount of 'freedom' made possible by the geography of Dartmoor which allowed practically no possibility of escape and offered a very bleak environment. It is evident from Walter's letters from this period that the prisoners were able to do quite a bit to enhance their cells and occasionally

33. Interior of punishment cell.

34. Interior of the chapel at Dartmoor.

to find ways to cheer up the meagre food rations. They ran the kitchens themselves and after an illicit late night fry-up of parsnips Walter confirmed to Tilly that Jack Ashley was 'queer'—that is, ill. This didn't surprise Walter who always distrusted fried food.

December 1917 was Walter's first Christmas away from home and despite the privations it turned out to be a spiritually inspiring one. He attempted to write creatively about his situation and although the result is a little stilted, it conveys the feeling of the moment:

> It is Christmas night and last night we celebrated Xmas Eve in a way that touched my imagination so I thought I would send on my impressions. Some 200 men representing different phases of religion decided to sing carols, a suggestion which was heartily taken up.
>
> What history is attached to Dartmoor that prison of prisons from which it is well nigh impossible to escape and which when clothed in winter's garment of snow reminds me of Siberia.
>
> The large, small windowed edifices called halls dominate Princetown and the original prison dates from the Napoleonic wars being mostly built by French prisoners of war. But what feet are they which now tread its slate landings and concrete basements these men who on Christmas Eve have dared to change as by a miracle the confining cells of despair into honeycombs of hope. As the resounding volume of power denoting strong lungs fills every corner of our hall, how one's heart beats. What words are

these?

> They shall be gentle brave and strong
> To spill no drop of blood but dare
> All that may plant man's lordship firm
> On earth and fire and sea and air.
> Nation with nation land with land
> Unarmed shall live as comrades free
> In every heart and brain shall throb
> The pulse of fraternity.

He then went on the describe the emotional impact of this shared attempt by the COs to combat their depressing circumstances:

> As if by magic the atmosphere of confinement is changed to liberty the semi-light of the gas jets appear as tongues of fire, the well conducted voices blend together in harmonies as triumph, and every word burns itself into ones fibre. The well learned words make it possible for the singers to face upward, and from above the sight of these men who have dared is unforgettable. Other hymns are sung proclaiming Peace on earth, good will to men, any resentment that one would expect to be present with at least some of the men, seems impossible in the atmosphere created.

> It was after visiting the various halls that at the gateway almost underneath the characters of Latin inscribed thereon, 'Parcere Subjectus', (Pity the Vanquished), the last halt was made.

> In deference to the varied countrymen present other than English, hymns were sung, and never before has Lead Kindly Light suggested such realities as at midnight in this Dartmoor mist. It was said by many that such an occasion was worth a prison experience. It will be a never dying experience in the minds of those present.

> There was no half-hearted resolution about these renderings determination was apparent upon the faces of the singers as the words of freedom and resolve came upon the midnight air.

> These things shall be a loftier race
> Than e'er the world hath known shall rise
> With flame of freedom in their souls
> And light of knowledge in their eyes[28]

It was a highly charged event to which the religious men would have been particularly susceptible after all their physical hardships and deprivations. Walter's next letter to his sister Tilly was on the 1 January 1918, (after the "Scotchmen kicked up a shindy at midnight as New Year is their special jollification night") in which he responds to her request for more detail about the Christmas events and atmosphere at Princeton:

Of course you not seeing inside the prison make it difficult for you to understand the effect prison has on one. Everything is so constituted to break the spirit of a law breaker, and Dartmoor is looked upon as one of the worst of its kind, being so far away from civilisation, and being a long term settlement also being an exception as work is done by the convicts outside, it being almost impossible to escape. Just think of Christmas celebrations inside a place which has such associations, nearly all the well known criminals of the last hundred years have spent time here, and we are in an atmosphere of spirit-breaking justice. Still the coming along of C.O.s have done miracles, no locks on doors, no armed guards, no chains, one warden has perhaps 100 or more COs in charge.[29]

It's interesting that he described this change in the way Dartmoor was being run as almost a moral effect of conscientious objection.

There are pipe lights in the halls, gas rings for heating food and it has been made very convenient, in many ways. These preliminaries I had to write so you could understand what my Xmas was like. There was not much doing apart from hundreds of parcels arriving till Xmas Eve, when some hundreds of men visited the various halls and sung hymns and carols. Some singing so I have never heard better. We had a Welsh conductor and was led by the male voice choir. I have sent Mr Wood an account of this which perhaps you will be able to read [this account is referred to in a later letter]. After this item there continued till the early hours of Xmas morning various collections of singers and musicians contributing towards the ushering if Xmas.

On Xmas day itself the chief business was visiting and as you walked round all the different halls you caught sounds of collective gatherings of friends, and numbers of the COs wives and youngsters were allowed in and I must add made a fuss of. The weather here was very wintry, cold and fairly deep snow. Each CO was allowed 6d by the H.O. [Home Office] but was not allowed the [actual] coin as it was thought it might be spent in goods which the outside public would want. What we got was anyway the vegetarian for Xmas dinner and this was the way the money was spent. Cheese pie, vegetables, celery, Bread, and Xmas pudding, so we didn't do so bad. To those who had things sent that required cooking the kitchen was open for supplying these needs. Fancy cracking nuts in a prison cell door. There was a great amount of liberality shown by the COs toward each other. Men went about asking if anyone had not received Xmas parcels and I had great pleasure in handing a box of cake nuts etc to a Norwich chap named Bradford[30] who lived in Newmarket St whose parents are dead. These being handed on to me for his benefit. On Xmas night a Concert of Folk Songs was given. The stage was made to look like an inn with the village celebrities present. The COs outside friends were given reserved seats and the hall was decorated and painted by a real artist (the story of this chap would take a letter by itself).[31]

It is an indication of the improved circumstances that the COs were allowed to go

35. Inscription on reverse: "Some artists at Dartmoor 1917. Second man from left was a tenor in Carl Rose Opera Co, a painter also." The names on the reverse are: far right Wiggins, front Willington and Smith, back row, Davies, Goulding, Shipp, Goulding, Cooley.

into Princeton itself.

>There was also on Xmas day numerous activities at the Hostel which is about five minutes' walk into Princetown. A good many had dinner there and I called in and saw Mr and Mrs Jimmy Rickes[32] were busy. The Norwich boys visited each other and some of them had jollifications together, the lights were allowed on till 12ocl and it was a sight to see the prison from the outside they don't worry about air raids here. On the whole it was a decent time but I'm afraid the things we had sent us made us think more of home.[33]

Notes

1. Possibly Edward George Roberts, listed on Peace Pledge Union website: Born: 1893, a London journalist and alternativist who was imprisoned in Wormwood Scrubs and then on the HO Scheme: Llandeussant Waterworks.
2. Possibly Arthur Read, listed on the Peace Pledge Union website as born: 1890, living at 43 Somerleyton Street, Norwich. His tribunal was in Norwich and he was on the HO scheme at Dyce and Penderyn. He was a starch maker, an alternativist and a Quaker.
3. Letter 6, 2 September 1917, WM to Tilly.
4. Ibid.
5. Ibid.
6. Ibid.
7. Percy Boddy.
8. William Theodore Newby, born 1894 and living at 21 Edinburgh Road, Norwich. He had been at Wormwood Scrubs and Maidstone prisons, was a Quaker, a Trade Unionist and an Absolutist. See the Peace Pledge Union list of COs.
9. An unknown Quaker woman—one of the many who supported the effort.
10. The No-Conscription Fellowship—an indication of the active roles women played in the NCF.
11. T. Bryan unknown.
12. H.F.S. Health Food Store.
13. Letter 7.
14. Pitman's Vegetarian Hotel and restaurant on Corporation Street, Birmingham.
15. Letter 7.
16. No details known, but E. Gilbert is on the Peace Pledge Union list of COs.
17. Rowlands—no details known, there are several Rowlands on the Peace Pledge Union list.
18. Letter 7.
19. Sadly, he left no record of these views.
20. Letter 7.
21. Letter of 6 October 1917.
22. Reel 4, IWM tapes.
23. Ibid.
24. Letter of 20 January 1918 to Annie.
25. Reel 5, IWM tapes.
26. Dartmoor History website https://www.legendarydartmoor.co.uk/2023/02/03/home-office-scheme/ accessed 17.02/23.
27. Reel 4, IWM tapes.
28. Letter 9, Xmas 1917.
29. Letter 10, 1 January 1918.
30. Not able to identify him.
31. Letter 10.
32. Unknown benefactors.
33. Letter 10.

6. New Year 1918–1920

Presumably work resumed immediately or soon after Christmas and two new matters took Walter's attention. The first was the arrival of a new prisoner.

> Yesterday [31 December] Mr Firth arrived unexpectedly from Maidstone [prison] and although I have been round to his room I have not seen him yet.[1]

And so began one of the better known and tragic stories of the COs.

Henry Firth was a thirty-year-old shoe-factory worker and Primitive Methodist[2] preacher, the eldest child of a large and poor family. As an Absolutist, he had been incarcerated in Wormwood Scrubs and then Maidstone prison for nine months until he became so broken by the treatment that he applied for the Home Office Scheme and was sent to Dartmoor. He has been erroneously identified by another CO (Mark Hayler—see below) as a Yorkshireman, but the Primitive Methodist website and the Peace Pledge Union list both make it clear that he was Norwich man— from the Sprowston Road.

36. William Henry Firth.

> As I write this letter Mr Firth has called round. He has asked me to say and also that you will convey these message if you can. W Newby[3] is very well exceptionally so, and said himself to Firth that he was quite happy. Tom Thorpe[4] is quite well and also Reggie Wild[5], and all three send their kindest remembrances to the NCF [No Conscription Fellowship] and hope the Social will be a success.[6]

From this one can gather that Tilly was involved in the No-Conscription Fellowship and fund-raising, and was in touch with other families. At this point Walter mentions Firth's health:

Mr Firth looks ill, he has the general appearance of the long termer but he will pick up after being here a short time. You can tell Mrs Firth he is lively and is being taken care of. The Norwich boys have taken him in hand. Mr Cracknell[7] wishes to be remembered to you.[8]

Walter then goes on to write about his other main concern of the moment and that was his prospects of being able to work outside the camps.

> ... In regard to the new scheme, we have not had official news yet and by what I hear I shouldn't be surprised if I went shortly to Buxton in Derbyshire as I hear some 100 or so are going. The new scheme rules are part good and part rotten. Still I expect you have read the newspaper side of it you know almost as much as I do, as you say there has been some discussion about it but no definite action has been decided yet. If only it was known what a waste this scheme is. I suppose we earn on average about 3½d each per week or less, so the loss to the country must be tremendous. Still as to myself I am much better in health this place is much more convenient than Talgarth and I am not sorry for the change. I wouldn't have missed Xmas here for a good lot, (outside being home). My 12 months is slipping away. Lots might happen in the meanwhile, we cannot be a long way off peace. The boys here are philosophical and numbers say they want to stop here till Peace is declared.

The relationship between his own family and his wife Jennie still seems distant. Jennie was neither a member of the Friends, nor overtly religious. But more importantly it seems fairly clear that she did not support her husband's views on conscientious objection added to which her loyalties would have been split since her brother Fred had been called up and was serving in the Royal Flying Corps, albeit in a desk job.

37. *Frederick William Swann in the uniform of the Royal Flying Corps in which he served as a clerk.*

By your account you had a quiet time at Xmas. I was glad Jennie came round [,] make her as comfortable as you can. You will think much the same as I do about her when you understand her. She is not any less religious because she don't show it the same as generally noticed.[9]

His next letter of 20 January 1918 is to his sister Annie, thanking her for sending a knitted balaclava helmet:

Dear Sister Annie and all

I was pleased to receive the note you sent me also the helmet which will come in handy in this inhospitable climate, still as the Americans say if you cant [sic] get through it you must climb it and that is what you have to do here, as the snow drifts instead of lay even as it does in Norwich, it has been know [sic] to almost cover the lamp posts and I have seen several drifts feet high across the roads. These wool helmets are just the thing for here as it is some cold. You will have the pleasure of knowing I shall be warmer because of it… It is certainly better here in many ways. Four days last week it was so bad that we were not allowed to work outside it was almost continually snowing and raining the whole of the week. Most of us were occupied in sewing mail bags. There is nearly always something going on and the time does not drag so much. It is difficult to think that six weeks have gone since I arrived.[10]

More recently there had been bombing on the coast, at Yarmouth:

Poor Tom Archer was upset a bit till he received news as his people at Yarmouth. They seem to have come through alright and I was pleased to hear Uncle Dick and all were likewise safe. They have had a time of it and I hope the report are true which we heard as it seems miraculous that no more lives were lost. Never before have I heard interesting things about Yarmouth such as Tom tells me, he and Uncle George were chums. It is curious how things work round.[11]

On Saturdays we generally prowl about together shopping he is pretty smart on bargains, his room is the best in the whole settlement, nicely decorated, floor polished, and he gathers ferns and makes brackets and pictures. Mine is next door and shows his up by contrast. I believe I shake the mat once a week and bed making I detest. We have to arrange bed clothes so they are aired every day. There has not been any men sent away yet on the new scheme but we expecting news every day.[12]

Walter was trying to get external employment under the new regulations:

In regard to what you mentioned about Mr Scott,[13] do I understand he said he would employ me on this land or not. It will be necessary for me to get work of national importance and if they will not allow me to do my own work I must get something which is suitable and convenient. The employers ideas will have a lot to do with it. I means as far as I am concerned so anything you hear about possibilities of work, you will let me know, I hear that clerks and shop assistants will not be allowed to take up the same work and business men will be allowed to go back if satisfactory to the Comm.[14]

Meanwhile the family kept the shop at White Lion Street open and trading—Jennie and Annie and perhaps some of the others were involved.

> Glad to hear you are going on well at White Lion St. I see that a licence has to be got to be able to open a business now so that those whose shop have been shut will have a chance, but I don't know whether this would mean COs businesses which have been closed.[15]

While he was hoping to find work outside the Camps, Walter continued with his stone cutting. The fact that he fared better than many may be down to his long standing interest in fitness, the legacy of the Victorian health cult which had inspired him, and when he went to prison was in good condition, or as he put it "I was a jolly good specimen in a way". The same could not be said for the new arrival, Mr Frith who, after nine months in prison, was probably quite literally half-starved. Nevertheless, he was sent with the Heavy Quarry Party to break stones in the extreme bitter weather. His condition worsened but when he went to the doctor he was accused of 'slacking' and sent back to work.[16] The evidence from Walter's letters seems to point to him being diabetic as well as malnourished. He was eventually admitted to the hospital at Princeton on 30 January.

Medical care was very limited, partly because of the focus on wounded soldiers and the lack of staff generally in the Work Camps, and partly because those doctors who did treat the COs were out of sympathy with them and gave only scant attention. In Firth's case he only received a milk diet after some of the COs intervened. Apparently, some eggs had been ordered for him but they didn't arrive in time.

> Jan 23 1918
>
> Dear Sister Tilly
>
> Just a line or two to let you know I am well and also a word or two about things in general. There is not much news, the men are getting ready for the new scheme and are expecting notice of removal. Jack Ashley tells me he is expecting to work on the land at Coltishall [a village on the Broads, north east of Norwich] and is calling at White Lion St to see Jennie and Annie to let her know how I am going on. He thinks he will get news of departure this week.

This would seem to indicate that Annie was working in the shop.

> For some little time I have guessed that Jennie has altered somewhat her ideas as to the Army and I have recommended her the book "I Appeal Unto Caesar". I am not certain of this but there are signs that make me think so. I have not tried to force her opinions on these things, I don't intend to I have too much Faith in the fact as to what is right for that but as I know you will be sometimes meeting her and that a certain amount of tact is needed you will understand what I mean.

This illustrates clearly that Walter and Tilly shared the Quaker religious tradition that Jennie had not been raised in.

> Glad to say I am as happy here as can be possible. I get much sympathy because of not having had leave, but sometimes I console myself that this is for the best as it gives J and I more time to think.[17]
>
> …
>
> Hope you are going on all right at 23. Do[18] Mr E [Alexander Eddington] ever talk to you does he mention me, did you mention to H Ward about young Palmer of Walcot who is here[19].

He goes on to talk about arrangements that can be made should he be called back to Norwich in an emergency—presumably he is thinking of the illness or death of a family member. He also mentions that he has not had a reply to his letter to Mr Wood. Considering that Wood was not entirely supportive of his position, he seems to have been quite patient with Walter.

The next letter is wrongly dated 1917, when it should be 5 February 1918, and it brings bad news about Mr Frith.

> Dear Sister Tilly
>
> Just a line or two.
>
> Poor Mr Firth is very ill in Hospital I have been to see him and he is seriously ill. They are wiring for his wife so I hear. Perhaps you will hear something about it, what we think is that he has diabetes so seemingly the food does no good. The committee here have taken his case up.

He then goes on to discuss the prospects for finding work outside and he keeps up an optimistic tone:

> Jack Ashley is having his case of the new scheme considered next month. The HOC [Home Office Committee] all seem to be keeping the men back for some reason as only about 10 out of 40 are being considered at present. They are down on agitators, we also hear Reggie Wild is ill in Maidstone prison. Glad to say I am well myself. You can guess I am thinking about my anniversary as it is twelve months this weekend since I left home. The time has gone quickly and it has been an experience you

bet. At present I am doing stonemasonry work which I like very well. Have not heard from Connaught Road lately you are not a good lot for writing regularly, but I will forgive you. Hope Ma & Pa are all well likewise Annie and yourself. The members are not very enthusiastic about the new scheme they think it was a dodge to keep men from joining the Flying Corps this Xmas. [possibly meaning escaping?][20]

38. *A group picture of the COs from Norwich at Princeton, Dartmoor 1917/18. Walter top left. Most probably taken at the time of Mr Frith's funeral.*

Then once again, he mentions the fact that Jennie is not receiving the kind of news that Tilly would have access to via The Society of Friends and the No-Conscription Fellowship:

> You perhaps think Jennie tell me all the news but there are many things she does not get to know about which you do. I believe I have spent the happiest times since I left home here this last few weeks. Fancy I have been here two months and although this is not a bright spot I like it better than any camp I have been to. It is much altered since I was here in April last things have settled down a bit and there are many boys I know. You can guess I make most of spare time reading etc. Some of the men are extraordinary. One we have who has a touch of religious mania, he reads the bible out loud at meal times and holds open air meetings. He asks the agent whether he is saved etc etc. All the Norwich boys are well. ... Hope you will be able to read this, but thought I would send anniversary remembrances to you I little thought when I left you 12 months would elapse like it has, but I am not downhearted and am still hopeful, my time

will come everybody's does who wait long enough. Give my love to Ma & Pa it would be a treat to see you all, still April will soon be here although the HOC may not treat me as I want to be treated. I cannot see them letting me go back to White Lion Street, still I shall have a try. Keep smiling

From your aff brother

Walter.[21]

Henry Frith died on 6 February, he was one of seventy COs who died in confinement. He was a slight young man from a very humble background but he was steeped in the Christianity of Methodism. Yet he suffered the full brunt of the prison regime and then medical neglect. A CO named Mark Hayler, who was working as an orderly in the hospital and looking after Frith, left an account, although the personal details about Firth are inaccurate:

> He was only a boy, 21, a preacher with the Methodists. I was an orderly at the hospital and I attended him. His wife came down from Yorkshire. I can see her now sitting outside his cell near the door. He had pneumonia. All the COs followed his coffin down to the little station—they couldn't prevent this.... It was all arranged by our own people. Some of us got hold of fog signals and put them on the line here and there. As the little train went out of the station...the signals went off, a sort of farewell. And I remember nearly a thousand men sang a hymn, 'Abide with Me.'[22]

The COs were not slow to make their outrage felt. Five hundred of them went

39. Carrying Mr Frith's coffin. It was a misty day.

on strike. Walter, never a trouble-maker, did not join them, but he was one of the coffin bearers—all of them Norwich men—taking the corpse to the railway station for its journey back to Norfolk.[23]

Walter's next letter describes the events:

> Friday
>
> Dear Tilly
>
> Have sent a short account of today's proceedings. The wave of indignation at the treatment of Mr Firth culminate in 714 men stopping work today, which was the day of the inquest. We are conveying the coffin in relays of men from here tomorrow Sat at 1.30 the H.O. [Home Office] paying £10 towards expenses. A solicitor was provided for Mrs Firth and death from natural causes was the verdict given by the coroner. Mrs Firth mentioned me when she was here and very reluctantly, I called and saw her, which I was glad of afterwards as she will no doubt tell you what she thought of me. Today has been full of incident this is the most unanimous proceeding since this has been a centre. Norwich boys are conveying the coffin to the station as bearers, most of the COs went without food all day so that the kitchen staff could come out. It was a very solemn service held in the afternoon hymns were sung and it was impressive, it has been historic. Mr and Mrs Riches took care of Mrs Firth and one of the Hobarts is leaving here tonight for Norwich with Mrs Firth, no doubt we shall have some penalty but it was a change to see such unanimous enthusiasm. There were some 300 men who worked a large number being engaged on necessary work like feeding stock and gas works.
>
> Walter.[24]

His next letters from 20 February 1918, again makes the best of things and says his health is much improved despite the damp.

> ... since I have been here I have taken up gymnasium again and you know how happy I am at that game. Since the funeral of poor Firth there has been a great deal of change in the Hospital here and much for the better. I hope you will see Mrs Firth. I was very glad to see her it was like a breath of Norwich air although I felt for her being on such an errand. Very glad Father is getting the allotment ready, I have got to like raw onions tremendously we also bake them here. There is one thing I ought to mention that is about the new scheme. Progress is terribly slow. Only four have left here there must be 600 and more eligible, they are only up to 700 or so and my number is 260 so I must not expect to get away very quickly. Also they have a knack of putting you off for six months for a very little offence, what I am looking for is PEACE. I am nearly sure they wouldn't let me come back to White Lion St. I've had enough navvying but

I would rather stick here a little longer and get FREEDOM. Yes, I think I feel more hopeful than I did. The idiots are losing their feet of clay and the sooner the better. Don't think by this letter that I am at all a rebel. I am still somewhat philosophical and am looked upon here as a drag upon the wheels of progress. You at Connaught Road have done wonderfully well I have appreciated your optimism more than once. I know how much you all must be fed up. I little thought on that snowy Sunday when I last saw you all that so much water would pass under the bridges and so much happen, but it has gone tremendously quickly. I am not a bit disappointed at the course things have taken they might have been much worse anyway I am happy because no one mourns because of me. You will know what I mean by this. Remember me to all who know me. We shall I hope all rejoice together in the very near future when a Peace which we shall appreciate will dawn upon Europe. I send love to Ma and Pa, and Annie and yourself.

Kiss Ma for me.
I remain
Your loving son and brother

Walter.[25]

Following Frith's death, the authorities eased up on the treatment of new COs arriving at Dartmoor:

You may or may not have heard that extra food is being provided in Prison for C.O.s also men arriving here are medically examined and given light work for a start. It would have made a great difference to me had that been in vogue when I arrived.[26]

But they also clamped down hard on men who had been part of the protest about his death, two were court martialed,[27] others had their pay docked and their rations drastically reduced. They were also penalised with regard to a new scheme coming in to release more men into working in the community if they could find jobs. Walter, who had not participated in the protest strike, was very keen to try again to get outside.[28]

As you can guess I am wondering about what's going to happen after my 12 months is up this comes due April 11th, as it is according to how they are treating others there will be no hurry and I am not counting much on what is likely to happen. Some have been on the scheme 18 mths and are still here so patience must be the watchword, the chief thing is for the War to be over any condition of release from here will not be as good as this and that is what we are looking forward to, much as I want to see all of you and you can only guess how much this is, I would endure this place a bit longer to see Peace declared.[29]

There was evidently some let up in the Scheme and men were being allowed home or perhaps to take up jobs in the community.

> Some of the Norwich boys will no doubt be coming home. One of the Holdens have [sic] already left and J Ashley will no doubt soon be coming. At present I am a mason and am getting used to using a hammer and chisel, it is rather hard work but I somehow like it. It is certainly interesting, if one's interest is in it is better work than I had at Talgarth. There are many things I should like to write about but don't know who's [sic] eye run over these pages before you get them.[30]

From the home front, Tilly sent news that their maternal grandfather in Yarmouth was ill and, then, that he had died. In Norwich little Walter, now 14 months old, had measles. Keeping morale up was a major effort—both for the relatives at home, and for Walter in Dartmoor:

> We keep an atmosphere of hopefulness going. Some do get downy which is likely to happen. Some have terrible troubles to meet, may have severed family connections, lost businesses, and many other troubles, but there are great compensations which will be apparent to you without any explanation.[31]

Religion and faith were what kept them going, or for the political COs, their belief in a better social order.

> There are many missionaries and ambassadors here if you are hazey on a particular branch of thought or religion you lay yourself open to enlightenment. They are all out for converts. Open air meetings inside the grounds are now the order.[32]

There were new seasonal work camps opening up:

> We hear large batches are going out on potato growing who that will mean and how many I do not know. It is said to be in Wales. Also names have been asked for house building near Glasgow. Somehow I would just as well remain here at present. As for the new Sch. The 18 mth men [men who have served 18 months] are now leaving and scheme is going slow. Why this is so is quite obvious to those who can put two and two together.[33]

This was presumably a punishment for the Frith protest, but Walter was concerned about the Conscription of Women Bill and how it might affect his family especially Tilly but he cannot say all he would like because of censorship. His tone about his hopes for peace became almost conspiratorial, "We watch for signs. They are appearing, and I am sure what we all wish for will come, because it must."[34]

On the practical side he was pleased that "a COs [sic] wife who is staying in Princetown washed and mended my stockings, which is a great help. I cannot darn somehow. I have got two pairs with no feet in, by the way is there any clothes of mine at Connaught Road, trowsers [sic], stockings etc. Somehow I don't think there is." This is a reminder of just how poor so many of the COs were—they had no means of obtaining sufficient clothes. But the local Quakers offered them probably the only comforts that they did obtain:

> Mr and Mrs Rickes are quite well. They get plenty of visitors they seem generally full up. I generally go round every Sunday. They have Fellowship meetings and we have a good time.[35]

Nevertheless, many of the Norwich men were homesick and Walter asks Tilly to send them a letter from the No-Conscription Fellowship in which she is involved. The men try to keep their spirits up: "We get some smiles here sometimes. There has been an epidemic of football matches, the different parties challenge each other, they are some games."[36]

As Walter recalled later in his IWM interview, coming to terms with prison life depended a great deal on your own personal attitude and determination but:

> The most difficult problems that you had to deal with were the things that were in your mind as to the kind of problems that your family had and your wife in regard to the children. I think that was the greatest thing you had upon you the thing you thought of most that was the problem.[37]

40. Hall 7 Football team at Dartmoor. Names unknown.

Letters were the only lifeline and he was able to keep his family reasonably well-informed of his condition, given the censorship. Of course, people outside the family had little interest in COs since their own circumstance were entirely caught up in the horrors and privations of the war and the terrible loss of life. The reverse was also true, the COs only had limited knowledge of how the war was progressing and how the civilian population was coping. There were no newspapers in the camps so they relied on what their relatives could tell them, or presumably, what they could glean when they went into Princeton.

After April 1918 there are no more letters extant. It's possible he was sent to other camps but what is known from his own testimony is that he suffered a severe injury while stone cutting at Dartmoor:

> Being placed in a stone masonry shed I had the experience of a sharp piece of stone which pierced my forearm and which because there was no

suitable medical help this was extracted with a tool that gave me untold agony.[38]

And this may have led to his successful application to be released from the camps and to his finding work outside.

In his interview he said that he managed a health food store in Birmingham for a year, this was probably Pitman's—a hotel, restaurant and health food store on Corporation Street.[39] The building still exists. Following that period,

> ... and still not being allowed freedom I was engaged as a gardener at Thorpe near Norwich. This was after peace had been declared. After all my experiences I felt no signs of humiliation as although I had passed out and was financially poor I was glad that I had survived and had proved my conscientious objection to be right.[40]

He was certainly fortunate in being able to get work since many COs were blighted by their war-time history and had great difficulty in surviving at all after the war. But he was evidently willing to turn his hand to anything useful. In 1920, through a contact made in Birmingham, he was able to arrange for a substantial sale of new stainless-steel cutlery to Roy's of Wroxham, a family-owned department store for the holiday boating trade, which was a rust-free improvement on what they had previously provided.[41] When exactly he was released is not known. His sentence had been five years and he probably served about two and half years. Certainly, he was not released until well after the armistice. While this was probably intended to be punitive, it was in parallel to the military demobilisation which only happened over many, many months, partly because of clearing up work to be done in France and Germany, and partly because of the fear of flooding the employment market at home. There simply weren't enough jobs, so COs were not likely to be favoured.

As far as the armistice itself went Walter noted in his IWM interview:

> When the Armistice was declared I think that everybody—either people who had been in the war itself and those that were against war—that was an exceptional time for them because the COs there [sic] ways of celebration could a little bit different, I mean, they didn't go to the nearest pub and get as much drink as they could—they didn't do that. But they joined in a kind of a heartfelt of [sic] there being this declaration 1918.[42]

In Britain the reaction to the armistice was very mixed. It ranged from jubilant celebrations on the streets to quiet sighs of private relief to deep despair and mourning for the horror and loss of life. It was quickly clear that there was no going back—although the main institutions of British government and society were still in place, life had changed beyond what anyone could have anticipated. There was a maw, a gap—before and after. The men who came home were damaged physically, mentally, spiritually; both traumatised and brutalised. They had become used to killing and some may even have come to enjoy it. The aggression that had been bred in Flanders came home and found outlets in other causes. Demobilised veterans were recruited to join the Auxiliary police (the Black and Tans) in Ireland. In England existing industrial unrest grew into Labour Wars that culminated in the National Strike. Opposing them were strike breakers and the emergence of the British Fascisti in 1923.[43]

The toll was both personal, social and economic. There was high unemployment and women had to be forced to leave the workplace to make way for the men. There was an enormous bill for disability pensions to be paid and there was a resentful division between those who had fought and those in protected jobs who had stayed at home in comparative comfort and managed to get on with some semblance of ordinary life. Ironically, this bitterness didn't always extend to COs. According to Walter's IWM interview he found that many returning soldiers were now far more inclined to agree with the cause of the COs than they had been and some wished that they themselves had taken a stand against the war that had proved so devastating.

Walter, as a former CO, was barred from voting in elections for 4 years, and didn't regain the franchise and thus full acceptance back into the community until the mid-1920s. As to what he felt about the experience, he had not changed his position and he felt that what the COs had suffered had been highly significant in the long term:

> ... since that time there have been more and more people against war than there were before, there were more and more people, the only thing that you can say about as to the what the COs did in the First World War was to really start a kind of an anti-war attitude and a kind of practical objection to it which will go on…should there be another war there will be people who will be Conscientious Objectors. That's what I think.[44]

He was not wrong but it took a while for that to happen.

Notes

1. Letter 10.
2. Primitive Methodism was a simpler more charismatic, and democratic form of Methodism that was popular among the lower classes.
3. Not able to identify him.
4. Not able to identify him.
5. Probably Reginald William Wilde.
6. Letter 10.
7. Not able to identify him.
8. Letter 10.
9. Ibid.

10. Letter 11.
11. Ibid.
12. Ibid.
13. Unknown farmer or horticulturist.
14. Letter 11.
15. Ibid.
16. Kramer, pp. 128-9.
17. Letter 12.
18. This use of 'do' rather than 'does', was Norwich dialect. For example: do yew now go ...
19. Letter 12.
20. Letter 13.
21. Ibid.
22. Ibid., in fact he was 30 years old and came from Norwich.
23. Reel 5 & 6, IWM tapes.
24. Letter 14.
25. Letter 15.
26. Letter 18, to Tilly, 25 April 1918.
27. C.H. Norman and S.L. Hughes, according to Letter 16.
28. Letter 16, to Tilly, 3 March 1918.
29. Letter 17, to Tilly, 11 March 1918.
30. Ibid.
31. Letter 18, to Tilly, 25 April 25 1918.
32. Ibid.
33. Ibid.
34. Ibid.
35. Ibid.
36. Ibid.
37. Reel 6, IWM tapes.
38. Ibid.
39. The first British health store was opened by James Henry Cook in Corporation Street, Birmingham in 1898. It was named after Sir Isaac Pitman who invented the shorthand system and was a well-known vegetarian.
40. Reel 6, IWM tapes.
41. Personal notes, perhaps for a talk or article, 'A Memorable Introduction'.
42. Reel 6, IWM tapes.
43. Hynes, Samuel, *A War Imagined*, pp. 354—6.
44. Reel 6, IWM tapes.

7. 1920–1937

It's safe to assume that Walter was back in Norwich by mid-year 1920 at the latest since his second son was born in March 1921 and was named Jack, possibly after Jack Ashley since Jack is not a Manthorpe family name. As with the sons of returning soldiers, Walter's first son, Walter Frederick, may have been startled and discomforted by the sudden appearance of a father whom he had never really known. While Jennie ran the shop, young Walter had been left much of the time with his dour grandmother whom he found very dreary and on one occasion, as a toddler, he was found making his own way through Norwich to find his mother at the shop. His earliest memory of his father was noteworthy. He recalled that as a child he had been given a toy gun and when his father came home and saw it, he seized it and broke it across his knee. This was a dramatic introduction to pacifism for a young boy and an indication that Walter senior was far from recovered from or reconciled emotionally to his experiences.

Norwich had lost 3,500 men and Norfolk had lost 12,000—a far higher proportion than other counties.[1] The reburial of Edith Cavell outside the cathedral on 15 May 1919 was a major civic event. Yet before people could move on, there was another catastrophe and that was the Spanish Flu of 1918–19 which swept through the army and navy towards the end of the war and spread from them into the civilian populations of Europe, the USA and then worldwide killing an estimated 50 million people. Both Walter and Jennie caught it but survived.

There was disagreement about a fitting war memorial that would represent the people of Norwich and it wasn't until 1926 that the Lord Mayor commissioned Lutyens to produce one of his last designs. In the early 1920s mourning and remembrance were running alongside a new sense of social awareness; plans were drawn up to clear the slums, create new suburbs of council housing, encourage health and provide recreation in the form of parks and sports facilities. At long last the working classes were to be included in the country's move forwards.

Keeping the shop going had been a very precarious endeavour and Jennie had needed the support of like-minded people. Fred Scott, the free-thinking architect, had lent them money at some point and that still had to be paid back. Ironically, one of the privations of war probably had a beneficial effect for Walter's embryonic health food shop in Norwich. The Defence of the Realm Act had brought in black-outs, press and postal censorship, and daylight-saving time but also prohibited the making of white bread and introduced rationing early in 1918 that went on into 1921. Sugar, meat, butter and cheese were all rationed but importantly for small shopkeepers, people had to register with one grocer and buy only from them. The Health Food Stores was a recognised supplier of rationed food, so, while rationing lasted it may have insured a loyal clientele.²

When he came home Walter was not slow to take strategic action in building up his business. He hired a stand at a Food Trades Fair, for the massive investment of £16, where he especially promoted the health value of olive oil. That he was rapidly accepted back into Norwich mercantile life is proved by the fact that he served as President of the Norwich District Grocers' Association from 1923–28.

From the beginning Walter had offered his customers advice on health and diet and he began to build up a small library of reference books. This resulted in him developing a dialogue with the local doctors through their patients. He was his own guinea pig and advertisement—giving up sugar to rid himself of catarrh, for example. Once he had recovered from imprisonment he looked fit and well so that being a vegetarian and a teetotaller was good for promotion of his wares.

41. Past president Norwich District Grocers' Association badge.

This personal approach meant that people took more interest in both the shop and the supplies and did not ask for credit in the way they did with other grocers. In an article he wrote in 1965 he noted the importance of personal commitment to the products he sold and the necessity for patience in building up the business and establishing a good reputation. He advised on the value of engaging with societies related to health and of being prepared to give talks locally. One of his talks, 'Diet and Health', explored the chemical and biological benefits of whole, natural and raw foods and expressed a faith in the psychological and spiritual benefits. He wrote that processed foods accentuate "our brutal qualities that fixes our actions upon a physical plane", whereas healthy foods "lift us into a higher mental atmosphere where physical contact such as warfare becomes unthinkable".³ This language has the flavour of Eastern mysticism. On the financial side he paid for supplies on delivery or in the shortest possible time to gain maximum discount benefits. He avoided borrowing from his bank but secured its help with purchasing goods from foreign countries. As an employer he said "Every consideration must be given to one's assistants and, if possible, as in my own case, a yearly bonus will help to encourage a sense of personal co-operation." He changed his shop

42. Walter and Jennie in the 1920s.

windows every week and took no notice of "the tactics of neighbouring shops" which offered discounts and "mass appeal". He stocked magazines and pamphlets about health issues to educate his customers. He rarely advertised but he did cater to particular needs—for example, Jewish dietary needs. He was an inveterate letter writer both to individuals and the press and took every opportunity to visit other health food stores and meet "leading personalities whose outlook and idealism was stimulating".[4] Many Quakers began to take up vegetarianism and there were a number of food provision companies—Mapleton's, Allison's and Pitman's—that were trusted. Muesli was invented and became popular, as did raw food diets. [5] Walter's Health Food Stores had a reputation for quality and he gave personal service as well as home delivery.

His views on health were firmly anchored in his religious beliefs and many years later he expounded on them:

> ... I will not recognise no other principle than that man, every man, can be united in faith to a Creator of perfection. A Creator who release all who have faith enough in the regeneration of himself, otherwise a belief that the spirit must animate the physical... Man is fearfully and wonderfully made and as time goes by so do all the theories which at certain times seem indisputable. One fact which is observable you can prove. Take very strong and healthy parents it is not a certainty that they have strong and healthy children hence Eugenics are not absolutely dependable. There is a greater factor in such things and that we label Love.[6]

He was part of an early initiative to start a retail association for health food grocers so that they could share information, ideas, and suppliers. As he wrote in an article later: "It has been said that Norfolk is not in England and, with my store being in Norwich, there was little opportunity for me to associate with other proprietors..."[7] The first attempt to remedy this was in 1924 with the Food Reform Traders' Association but this was short-lived due to lack of support. In 1931 The National Association of Health stores was founded in London and had a national membership of 37, and two years later in order to give the members limited liability, Health Stores (Wholesale) came into being and held regular meetings. Walter became an acting member and then President of the National Association of Health Stores. The members advertised themselves with this message:

> Health Stores have for many years been advocating and facilitating the adoption of a vital natural diet. By purchasing your supplies from any of the undermentioned establishments, you will not only be assured of obtaining foodstuffs of guaranteed quality, purity and integrity, but you will be helping to support the much needed educational work which they, hand in hand with the great pioneers of Natural Therapeutics, are doing to eradicate disease and to inaugurate an era of universal health and happiness.

It must surely have been a message that people wanted to hear as they recovered from the traumas of the Great War.

It was a Norwich man, R.H. Mottram, who was one of the very first authors to write about his war time experiences with his best-selling *The Spanish Farm*, published in 1924. It described the conflict from a civilian perspective in Flanders and drew on his own work as a reparations' assessor. Mottram was a protégé of John Galsworthy and the book reflects on the mundanity and inanity of war in a measured way. D.H. Lawrence wrote less dispassionately of the barbarising effects of the war on the home population. In *Kangaroo* he pointed an accusing finger at the Jingoistic press, the base politicians and the "stay-at-home bullies" who between them produced what he called a "reign of terror" at home.[8] Lawrence perceived that something had changed in Britain that could never be recovered and many other writers took up a theme of loss and nostalgia. Michael Arlen's, *The Green Hat* also became a best-seller but, in contrast, this was the original 'gay young thing' novel that presented the cynical, desperate and dissolute society of London in the wake of the war. The books that really presented an anti-war point of view didn't emerge until late in the decade and two that had a major impact were Robert Graves' *Goodbye to All That* (1929) an officer-class rebellion against the old order and Erich Maria Remarque's *All Quiet on the Western Front* (1928/9) describing the physical and moral degradations of war from the point of view of a lowly soldier on the German side. The latter book was on my grandfather's bookshelves.

The No-Conscription Fellowship was wound up in 1919 but just two years later it was succeeded by a new organisation called the No More War Movement chaired by the pacifist and socialist Fenner Brockway. It had international links and attracted some leading figures including Albert Einstein.[9] The Fellowship of Reconciliation which had been founded in 1914 and was a Christian organisation with a large Quaker membership, continued with George Lansbury and Donald Soper, a high-profile Methodist and charismatic speaker, among the leading lights. In 1919 the Women's International League of Peace and Freedom emerged out of the International Women's Congress which had campaigned against the war since 1915. War Resisters' International was founded in the Netherlands in 1921 with offices in London. As part of the Paris Peace Treaties of 1918 the axis powers formed The League of Nations Union, while not absolutely pacifist, it promoted international peace and co-operation. It was an organisation to which individuals could subscribe and, in the 1920s and 30s, it represented one of the greatest hopes for the future.

However, it was not until about a decade after the armistice that people who had supported the recent war really began to re-assess its impact. It was this reaction that produced a proliferation of peace associations. The Church of England launched a 'Christ and Peace' campaign in October 1929 and the Lambeth Conference in the following year proposed that war was incompatible with the teaching of Jesus Christ.[10] Peace Fellowships and Peace Societies sprang up in many churches of all dominations. These in turn formed youth groups and held conferences.

Most notable among the crusaders for peace was Dick Sheppard, vicar of St Martin's-in-the-Field, London. He became a pacifist in 1927 and, in an attempt to regain the reputation of the Church of England, which had been badly damaged, to say the least, by its militant support for the war, he founded The Peace Pledge Union in 1933. With offices all over the country, it was one of the most influential peace organisations based on the simple idea that people would sign a pledge, just as they did for temperance, to give up war and promote peace. The very

43. Walter and Jennie in their back garden 1926.

simplicity which made it popular was also politically naive.

During this period Gandhi, who had been influenced by Tolstoy's pacifism, was demonstrating the power of civil disobedience in India and this, too, made people hopeful for a new way of solving conflict. As has often been noted, Gandhi had some advantage in being up against the British Empire which allowed dissent and criticism at home. Even though there was cultural anxiety about war, at this point no one was anticipating the criminal savagery of the Nazis. People were trying to put their lives back together.

Striving to better themselves but stay within their modest means, Walter and Jennie stayed in the same small terrace house all their married life. It's an indication of how hard they worked as a team that they were able to educate their sons, and dress the boys very well if the photographs are anything to go by. Young Walter obtained a place in the new grammar school at Eaton—the City of Norwich School; Jack, who was less academic, attended C.N.S. junior school and then went on to a small private day school, Bracondale. Both boys followed their father in being sporty: hockey for Walter and football for Jack. Both cycled, and eventually sailed too and were generally robust and brought up on a healthy diet although not exclusively vegetarian, but wholemeal bread and unrefined foods were fundamental. They exuded vitality. Neither were vaccinated for smallpox or anything else. Walter Senior's ambition for his elder son was that he should become a professional with all that meant in terms of social and educational elevation.

By the early 1930s the children that had been born during or soon after World War I were growing up and reading the recently-published memoirs and poetry of the survivors and commentators. The full horrors of the war were now in the public domain given voice largely by an educated middle class. Siegfried Sassoon's war poems and his *Memoirs of an Infantry Officer* (1930) and Vera Brittain's *Testament of Youth* (1933) were some of the most notable. They had a big cultural impact: any remaining illusions of glorious victory were shattered; people who had supported the war began to feel guilty. Pacifism gained new energy both as an ideal amongst the young and as a strand in public life.

In 1931 Japan invaded Manchuria bringing a real fear of a new war but not of what it might be like; as Ceadal has pointed out, English pacifists were largely or even completely ignorant of Japanese warrior culture. Various strains of pacifism and *pacificism* (an absolutist position) were emerging—some humanitarian, some religious; some more socialist than pacifist and vice versa. In 1931 there was a War Resisters' Triennial Conference in Lyons and in the following year there was a World Disarmament Conference in Geneva at which Albert Einstein called for a complete cessation of the manufacture of munitions. In 1932 a former suffragette formed a new Peace Army with the idea of 'men of goodwill' forming a human barrier between opposing forces (800 people subscribed) and there was a World Anti-War Congress in Amsterdam. A great deal of talking was going on and there

PEACE or WAR?

A National Declaration on the League of Nations and Armaments

NATIONAL DECLARATION COMMITTEE, 15, Grosvenor Crescent, S.W.1.

TO MEN AND WOMEN OVER EIGHTEEN.

Will you please answer overleaf these five questions:—

1. Should Great Britain remain a Member of the League of Nations?

2. Are you in favour of an all-round reduction of armaments by international agreement?

3. Are you in favour of the all-round abolition of national military and naval aircraft by international agreement?

4. Should the manufacture and sale of armaments for private profit be prohibited by international agreement?

5. Do you consider that if a nation insists on attacking another the other nations should combine to compel it to stop by
   (*a*) economic and non-military measures;
   (*b*) if necessary, military measures?

These questions are put to you as a means of showing to our Government and to the world where Britain stands as to Peace and the Price of Peace.

We want your answers whether "Yes" or "No," with or without explanation or commentary.

A leaflet will be supplied in which you will find the guiding considerations which, in our view, should be kept in mind when answering the questions.

Kindly hand this Ballot Paper to a collector, who will call in a day or two.

Published by the National Declaration Committee, 15, Grosvenor Crescent, S.W.1. and printed by King & Jarrett, Ltd., Holland St., Blackfriars, S.E.1.

44. The League of Nations Union ballot paper.

was a trend for anti-war plays and 'next war' novels.[11]

And then, in 1933, Hitler came to power and with him came the sense of a real and terrible threat. To many people Non-Violence no longer seemed like a good defence. It was at this point Walter senior chose to tell his eldest son that he had been imprisoned as a conscientious objector in World War I which was presumably the start of the family conversation about pacifism, although the basic precepts were already in place since Walter senior's whole life bore witness to his beliefs.

In 1934/5 the League of Nations Union, a national membership network which had been set up to support the ideals of the League of Nations, introduced a countrywide Peace Ballot with five questions to encourage people to think about and support a programme for peace. The LNU activists were largely well-educated and well-connected but they came from across the political spectrum.[12] In Norwich, the ballot took place between 12 and 24 November 1934. Over fifty percent of the electorate in Norwich participated (more than 10% higher than the national average for general elections) and the questions were aimed at raising the discussion on just how much people would support peace initiatives, which ones, and at what political stage might they support a war. It was a kind of weather vane on pacifism. The results were an overwhelming support for the League of Nations, for a reduction in armaments internationally and nationally, and showed a preference for economic and non-military methods for solving disputes. However, there was still quite strong support for military measures if absolutely necessary.

In 1935, young Walter was 18 and he began a new diary for the year. He had already left school and his father had paid for him to be articled to Arnold, Son & Hedley Chartered Surveyors, Land Agents and Auctioneers and Fire Loss Assessors at 9 Princes Street, Norwich. The partners were Harry H. Arnold, Algernon F. Arnold and Hubert F. Hedley. The everyday bread-and-butter work included fire damage surveys and small building projects such as a new post office in Aylsham, shops on the Aylsham Road in Norwich (which Walter designed), and a boot factory in Sprowston. The Halifax Building Society came to them for all their dilapidations and repairs. Although there was a lot of office work, there were also many days out driving all over Norfolk—Walter at the wheel as he had recently learned to drive—looking at various sites. More excitingly there was building work for some of the big Norfolk landowners and this gave Walter a glimpse of a new and more glamorous world. As a land agent, Harry Arnold knew his way around the estates of aristocrats and landed gentry—Heveningham, Honingham, Leatheringsett, Raveningham, Rainthorpe—and was invited to shoots and would sometimes take Walter with him. He also knew his way round the auction houses and would himself buy properties for resale to turn a profit. When they went out for a day's surveying, they would have lunch or tea at a big hotel, or he might bring a hamper of food and champagne which impressed young Walter.

His evenings were spent at lectures, concerts, 'the flicks' and especially at

45. *Young Walter aged about 19.*

the Maddermarket Theatre either in the audience or later as a 'player'. The Maddermarket Theatre had opened in 1921 and was the first permanent recreation of an Elizabethan Theatre founded by Nugent Monck who had worked with William Poel. Poel was the first to restore Shakespeare's plays with the full text and to play them in the Elizabethan style without elaborate scenery. The Maddermarket was an amateur dramatic society but with an experienced professional management and highly thought of, not just in Norwich. George Bernard Shaw, the noted vegetarian, socialist and pacifist, sometimes let his new plays be performed there

46. Taking the CSI exams in London 1930s.

soon after opening in the West End.

Walter also had a circle of friends with whom he was often out and about. One close friend was Geoffrey Crane, who, at that time, worked for the Castle Street ironmongers, Johnson Burton and Theobald, and who lived near Eaton Park. Later he spent a good deal of time with Jack Brockway, also training to be a surveyor. Brockway lived at Coltishall where they learned to sail together. He also had girls whom he took out or met up with regularly—an 'M' in 1935, and an 'A' in 1936 are regular entries in his diary.

47. May 1935, a sketch of young Walter with new glasses painted by a work colleague.

In March 1935, he went up to London for the first time to take some of his CSI exams and stayed with his Uncle Fred Swann and his wife at their home on Abbey Road.

Walter was an avid theatre goer and took in Gielgud's *Hamlet*, George Robey as Falstaff in *Henry IV Part 1*, *Life Begins at Oxford Circus* at the Palladium and Flannagan and Allan. Back in Norwich he was cast as Shylock in *The Merchant of Venice*. Jack was still at school and Walter went to see his school play and to a 6th form dance at C.N.S.

Often at weekends he would drive his parents out to the country or the coast either for the scenery or to visit relatives and presumably to practice his driving. They had some friends called Boswell at Barton Turf who gave him a series of books on architecture and building which must have provided the start of his later comprehensive collection.

In May the King's Silver Jubilee was marked with civic celebrations on Mousehold Heath. On 18 May Walter drove Harry Arnold out see The Pleasance at Overstrand—a house that had belonged to Lord and Lady Battersea. Years later he recalled that it was a salutary lesson in valuation. Harry Arnold looked all around the property and decided simply on the basis of the external architectural salvage, decorative stone and pottery items in the gardens, and without regard to the house, that it was worth buying, which he did for £5,000 later in the month. At around the same time Walter learned that he had passed the first level of his CSI exams.

In July he and Jack Brockway hired a boat for a week's sailing on the Broads. In Wroxham they met two girls from London and spent some time with them. During August he taught himself to swim, prepared particulars for the guest house at the Overstrand property and drove his family around. His father went up to London monthly for meetings of The National Association of Health stores and possibly also the Grocer's Association. The rhythm of Walter's young life in provincial Norwich was pleasant and steady and he had every good prospect ahead of him as he set his sights on London.

On 21 September Walter noted in his diary that Mussolini had rejected the peace proposals submitted by the League of Nations in the Abyssinian dispute. At the end of the month he attended the opening of the new Theatre Royal in Norwich—a performance of *White Horse Inn* with a free souvenir programme. On 3 October he wrote in his diary that Italy had invaded Abyssinia.

He was up in London again in the autumn for his studies and saw Gielgud's *Romeo and Juliet* at the New Theatre and also, with Brockway, *1066 and All That* at The Strand Theatre. He turned 19 in November and in December he went to see *Lady Precious Stream* at the Maddermarket. On 20 December Brockway phoned up to say that he had passed his exams. Christmas Day the family drove to Yarmouth, probably to see family members, Old Hamilton spent Boxing Day with them. Luckily for Walter he was invited to a party on 27 December and spent the evening with friends. In the New Year, 1936, things continued much the same. He did a lot of office work and evenings spent 'swotting'—he was very assiduous in his studies and obviously keen to get his qualifications. He was still seeing girlfriend 'A' quite often. Mrs Arnold invited him to dinner, a sign of approval at work. On Tuesday the 21st he sat up late listening to the wireless as news of the king's declining health was broadcast—"moving peacefully towards a close". The next day the King's death was announced and the Prince of Wales became Edward VIII, a fact that 'proclaimed over all England' two days later on 24 January.

In February Walter went to see G.B. Shaw's play *The Simpleton of the Unexpected Isles*—a satirical Utopian story set in the south seas. But most evenings he was studying. He went with the Architectural Association to visit the new Brooke House, built by S.J. Wearing in an art deco style for Eric Mackintosh, of the chocolate manufacturing family.

On a March trip to London he saw Robert Donat in *Red Night*—the first mention of an anti-war play. And he took his exams. After which he went to see Scotland play England at Twickenham. He resumed acting at the Maddermarket with a role as 'Digby' in *Last Voyage*, and on 5 April recorded:

> Anne's [A] to tea in pm and evening. This is apparently the anniversary of our meeting. Perhaps 12 months is long enough.

Plays at the Maddermarket usually ran from a Friday night 'Bills' night for members[13] and friends, through the following week. There were often parties or get-togethers in the evening and Walter senior always stayed up until his son came home, and Walter noted in his diary what time he arrived. On 25 April he didn't get home until 1.00am which evidently caused parental ire - he wrote "Dad very wild". Soon he heard that he'd passed the second tranche of exams. In March 1936 Harry Arnold wrote to Walter Senior to say how well he thought Walter would do in his career and how he would suit an "old-fashioned private firm and then on to a public appointment". That proved an astute assessment. At the end of the month 'A's mother ticked him off for his forward behaviour (presumably physical advances) and he was banned from seeing 'A' again. Perhaps just as well. The paper came through from the CSI for his next and final set of exams. He began rehearsals for *The Shoemaker's Holiday*. He was working at Brundall, a village just east of Norwich, setting out building sites on the garden estate. He had another late-night walking with friends in Eaton Park, which seems to have been a favourite venue. He arrived home tardily and once again "Dad went wild". Walter was outgrowing the family environment.

In July he took a week's holiday to visit the new theatre at Stratford where he saw

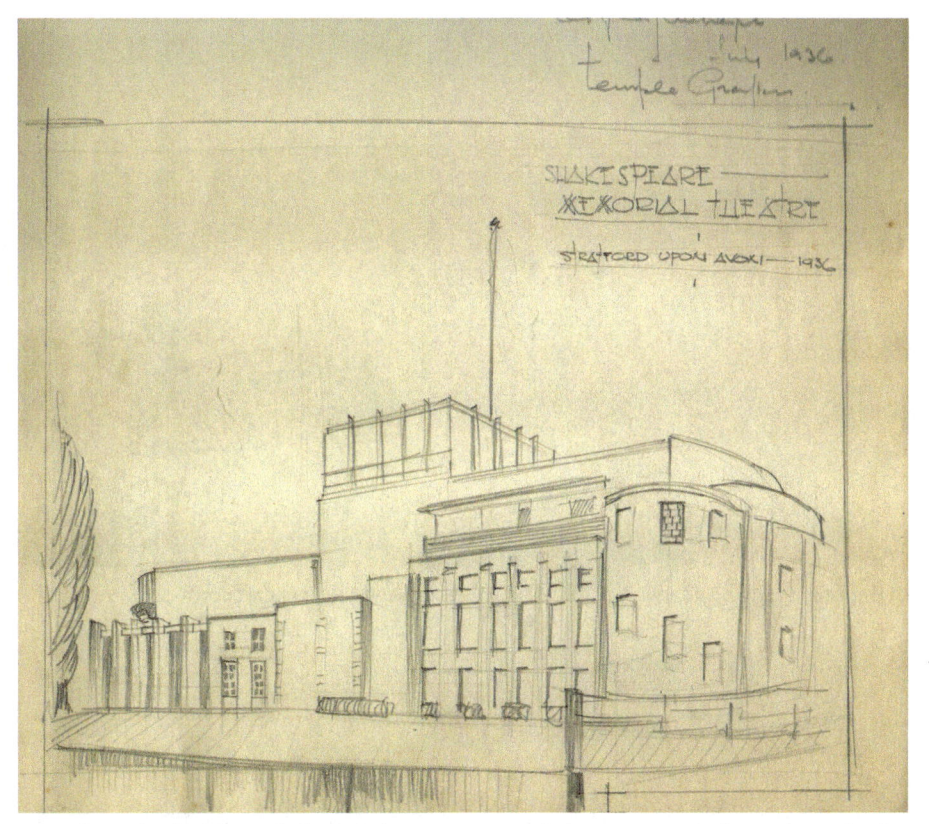

48. *Walter's sketch of the newly-built Shakespeare Memorial Theatre at Stratford-upon-Avon dated 1936.*

Twelfth Night and *Romeo and Juliet*. He annotated his programme that the actor playing Romeo was effeminate and evidently did some sketching.

There are no more entries for 1936 and his diary for 1937, (if there was one) has disappeared. But these were heady times and three things of importance to his outlook occurred that year. First, he was given a small part in the Maddermarket's November production of W.H. Auden and Christopher Isherwood's *The Ascent of F6*, the story of a mountain climber who is destroyed by his ambition. This was the first provincial production of the play after its London debut in May and Walter was always proud of his involvement. The play includes the first comic version of what was to becomes the famous Funeral Blues lament (*Stop all the clocks…*) and music by Benjamin Britten.[14]

Second, at some point between 25 May and 25 November, to celebrate Walter's 21st birthday, Walter senior took the family to Paris for the Exposition Internationale des Arts et Techniques dans la Vie Moderne (International Exposition of Art and Technology in Modern Life). This impressive and innovative Expo was a valiant attempt to promote peace in Europe and provided a significant

114   Different Drums: One Family, Two Wars

49. Walter beside the Seine with the exhibition and the Soviet pavilion in the background, 1937.

50. Walter in front of the Place de Varsovie, Paris 1937.

educational opportunity for Walter. Some of the great modern architects had designed pavilions including le Corbusier for France's Pavilion of New Times. The Spanish pavilion provided the first public exhibition of Picasso's vision of the horrors of war, 'Guernica'. Albert Speer's German Pavilion complete with eagle and swastika, faced and challenged the Soviet's mighty building crowned by outsize heroic statues of a male industrial worker and a female farm operative. Britain had underestimated the exhibition's importance; the project was underfunded and their pavilion eschewed modernism in favour of arts and crafts. The whole exhibition represented not just the excitement of new design and technology but also the character of the nations represented.

Third, 1937 also saw the publication of Huxley's *Ends and Means* a series of essays which formed *An Enquiry into the Nature of Ideals and Into the Methods Employed for Their Realization*. Aldous Huxley, a philosopher and novelist, was an active member of the Peace Pledge Union and his works of both fiction and non-fiction essays reflect his interest in the structuring of societies, pacifism, universalism and mysticism. *Ends and Means* was a tremendously influential book for all those who were inclining towards pacifism. Walter's copy survives. Huxley was interested in large scale social reform and felt that cultural circumstances could modify human nature, but that the problem of evil could only be challenged by individual will. He believed that monotheism had been abandoned for the idolatry of nation, class and even the individual. While he looked for solutions to society's ills his main point was that how people accomplished their ideals would dictate where they ended up. The ends never justified the means—they couldn't because through dishonest, corrupt or violent means you would reap very different ends than intended. Here at last was a logical indictment of war.

Notes

1. Browning, p. 118.
2. 'Health Food Trader' article No 53, November 1964.
3. Text of a talk 'Diet and Health'.
4. In 1971 he wrote to the Earl of Leicester regarding the disappearance of Canadian Geese at Holkham and advising that it might be caused by the disposal of chemical waste from the potteries into the lake. Lord Leicester wrote to thank him for his suggestion and changed the arrangements forthwith, letter 3 December 1971.
5. Spencer, Colin. *The Heretic's Feasts: A History of Vegetarianism*, 1995.
6. Letter, 14 April 1942 WM to WFM.
7. From article *The Early Struggle to Form a Retail Association* by W. Manthorpe in 'Health Food Trader' 1965.
8. Quoted in Hynes, Samuel. *A War Imagined: The First World War and English Culture*, 1990, p. 347.
9. Kramer, p. 12.
10. Ceadal, p. 68.
11. Ibid. pp. 89-93.

12. 'Theo Scott and the Norwich Peace Ballot of 1934' by Judith and Derek Merrill, in *Aspects of Norwich* Spring 2022 edition, published by the Norwich Society.
13. For people who put up posters or 'bills' to help promote the play.
14. W.H. Auden had attended Gresham's School in North Norfolk.

8. January 1938—February 1939

On 8 January 1938 Walter, then 21 years old, left the employ of Arnold Son & Hedley where, he wrote in his diary, he had 'received so much good instruction and had so many enjoyable days.'[1] On Monday the 10th he began work in London at the Directorate of Lands and Accommodation in Her Majesty's Office of Works. His first explicit mention of Youth House, the vegetarian hostel where he was to live, is on 21 March 1938 but it seems likely he stayed there at or soon after his arrival in January since the notes in his diary are to do with play rehearsals for *You Never Can Tell* by George Bernard Shaw and also 'Weekend Service' which seems to relate to duties at Youth House. On 2 February he noted that "Dad comes up", presumably to see how he was settling in. The following weekend his friend Geoff Crane came up for a visit, too. On 21 March he was meeting 'Mary' at Y.H. at 7.30pm. Mary,[2] who seems to have been a little older than the rest of the group and already married, became a close friend and confidant over next two years.

The origins of Youth House lay in the Federation of British Youth Movements that grew up after World War I. The Federation included the Young Friends (Quakers), the Woodcraft Chivalry, The Kibbo Kift, the Fabian Nursery, the Youth Section of the No More War Movement, the Young Experimenters, the Socialist Guild of Youth and the Practical Idealists Association. Among these many youth groups was The Guild of the Citizens of Tomorrow, organised in 1918 by the Theosophical Society for its 16-30 age group. The main activities of the Guild were in the arts, particularly pageants, plays and dramatic representations of belief, and co-operative summer camps.

In the mid-1920s The Guild had proposed a 'Youth House' scheme to provide a centre for

51. Programme of a pageant called The Light of Youth.

its own activities and for a central office and assembly rooms for the work of the Federation. Funds were raised and a Limited Liability Company incorporated in 1927. The objectives of the Company were to provide:

1. An educative experiment in Community Life based on the Ideal of Service and the other principles of the Foundation Document.

2. A meeting place for Youth of all nations.

3. Opportunity for the self-expression of Youth along their own lines through the acceptance of Responsibility.

4. Opportunity for Youth to re-educate themselves by study and research.

The founders included several Theosophists: Mrs Elsie Mitchell known as 'Mike' and Mrs M.V. English known as 'Lucifer' (both nick-named after archangels), Margaret Lane (Pan) Gerard Reilly (Nunc), Commander Dermot Cather, Mr Gregson (Greg) and Ursula Grundy. Other early founding figures included Bernard Banfield and his brother-in-law the architect Frank Jackman, and also Richard Titmuss; none of these three were involved in Theosophy. Bernard Banfield was connected to the Society of Friends and Richard Titmuss was an economist and Liberal social reformer and, later, one of the founders of the Welfare State.[3]

After a considerable search, suitable premises were found at 250 Camden Road in north London, a double-fronted villa built around the mid-19th century. The Guild decided to purchase it and turn it into a hostel.

Frank Jackman undertook the conversion of the premises and by sub-dividing rooms the house could accommodate twenty-two residents including staff in small bed-sitting rooms although there were only two bathrooms. There was a large hall, equipped for dancing, plays, lectures and table tennis plus a common

52. Youth House, exterior. 250 Camden Road, London.

room furnished with leather chairs and sofas in traditional club style. The kitchen and restaurant were in the basement. The restaurant served vegetarian meals to residents and also to non-residents at a slightly higher price.

53. *The common room at Youth House.*

54. *Dining room of Youth House. Date: Christmas early or mid-1930s.*
Two women sitting centre of picture are Winifred Shields and Maud (?). The man sitting front right is Nunc Reilly, one of the Theosophist founders.

The governance of the community was conducted on co-operative lines with residents and staff participating. Residents were expected to help out with domestic chores and the organisation of events. Financial control stayed with the board of the company.

The international club, that was open to non-residents, proved popular but the hope of Youth House acting as a hub to other youth groups did not materialise. It remained a single entity although eventually the Federation of British Youth Movements, (after World War II known as the British Youth Council) did make its headquarters there and initiated the International Youth Tramps and played an important part in establishing the Youth Hostel Movement in 1932.

In her biography of her parents, Richard Titmuss' daughter, Anne Oakley, commented that "The theme of youth having to take on, singly handedly, the task of fighting war and building peace was a common one at the time."[4] And certainly the generation that entered Youth House seem to have been thoroughly preoccupied with political and moral issues even though their jobs and social life were also very important to them. Richard Titmuss, born in 1907 and therefore at least ten years older than the residents of Youth House, was already dedicated, ambitious and tireless in his work via statistics and economics towards nationwide social improvement.

From the start the atmosphere was convivial, tolerant and intellectually lively while the environment was comfortable and homely. Internationalism and good-will to all nations were the leading ideals. "There was no religious, sex nor colour bars."[5] From the beginning there was strong emphasis on and involvement with peace movements and conferences. Conscription was a considerable barrier to progress in this area and discussed in a Youth House Magazine article of 1931, pointing out that in France the penalty for evading conscription to national service was 28 years in prison.

Notable among the early residents were the philosopher

55. *Youth House magazines and a pamphlet from The World Youth Peace Conference of 1928.*

and spiritual teacher Jiddu Krishnamurti[6] and V. K. Krishna Menon, one of the champions of an independent India. To meet the needs of young people the social side of the House was vibrant and many friendships and romances blossomed.[7] There were dances, plays, concerts, lectures, language classes, morning meditations as well as more informal games, debates and discussions. Topics for talks included Civil Liberties, the Howard League, Poverty and Population, Animal Welfare, and the Whiteway Colony. Sympathetic speakers included Michael Foot talking about the Labour Party and Michael Tippett on music. Youth House provided what single young people needed—a stable but open community with a flow of new faces and plenty of activities and company. Weekend camps, rambles and all-night country walks were a regular part of the activity programmes. The young people it attracted were generally office workers, civil servants or young professionals, foreign students particularly Indians studying at London University, and people with artistic interests.

56. *Marjorie Hutchinson, Louie Grimm and Jane (?) working in the kitchen at Youth House.*

By the mid-1930s, the members of Youth House were pursuing their efforts for international good-will under the darkening shadow of fascism in Europe. In March of 1938 the German Wehrmacht (the armed forces of the Third Reich) crossed unopposed into Austria. Hitler effected a Nazi take-over, the Anschluss, by an enforced plebiscite on 10 April in which Austrians voted for their own annexation under pain of losing their jobs or their lives. Undeterred, the British Prime Minister, Neville Chamberlain continued with his policy of appeasement.

In June Walter's diary includes a lecture on 'Unknown Dimensions' (presumably a Theosophical theme) and a number of garden parties. He also attended readings and rehearsals for G.B. Shaw's *Back to Methuselah*, a series of allegorical stories about the ills of Western society and how they might be addressed by people living longer and being able to impart a deeper experience. Walter went home to Norwich some weekends and by July he was taking advantage of Youth House's International Youth Tours organised by James Haynes Dixon, who worked for the Ministry of Transport and had started his own travel company based in the Strand.[8] Walter made a 4-day trip to Koln via the ferry to Ostend and may even have been acting as a courier for Dixon—something he certainly did after the war. He seems to have had time on his hands and visited an airport and sat at a café watching the planes arrive; he was always interested in mechanics and motoring. He took a night crossing and was back in Victoria Station at 7.30am on the 20 July and at the office at 10.00am.

There are no entries for August—a time when Youth House was opened up as a hostel for international visitors (one shilling a night) and the main hall filled with bunk beds to accommodate them.

57. *Members in the garden of Youth House. Exact date unknown.*
Back Row (from left): Tom Miller(?), George, an American Hart(?), Doreas Alan, Dorothy Hutchinson, Robert Buckingham, Walter Manthorpe – gesturing, perhaps this was the theatre group. Middle Row, seated: Margarite Sorso, Joan, Hans, Anne Parker. Front row: Elfreda, Lottie Schneider, Ted (Jeffrey?).

On 14 September Walter made the first mention of my mother Anne Parker, a clerk in the civil service who lived close by in Camden Square: "dinner with Anne at 6pm". There were more rehearsals and a reception for the 'Curtain Players'— the name of the Youth House drama group. A few days later he had dinner with his German friend Ernst[9] at the Vegan Restaurant. But Walter had to stay late at the office "owing to the international crisis". Hitler was demanding the transfer of the Sudetenland from Czechoslovakia to Germany and was on the point of invasion. The British and French policy of preserving peace was based on reasons that C.L. Mowat in *Britain Between the Wars 1918-1940* deemed "were not disreputable"[10] because France and Russia were weak in air power and geography alone prevented France (or Britain) from assisting Czechoslovakia directly.[11] France and England attended a conference with Germany and Italy in Munich on 22 September.

There must have been a meeting or lecture at Youth House the day before because on 22 September Walter's friend, Mary, who seems to have been a civil servant in the Post Office and a committed pacifist wrote to him in terms that give an idea of his unsettled mental state at the time:

> You know that I have so often listened to you before - but never, until last night, have I felt you to be really in need of a little sympathy and understanding. Then at the end of the evening your nervous distress over 'to go or not to go' to Morley[12] really worried me. So, tho' knowing you, I felt that your distress might be very temporary, I feel also that a few words from me might help.
>
> ...
>
> One small piece of advice — Don't let your good nature lead you in to too many things from which you will learn nothing — only give your knowledge to others. You are still too young and have so much to learn yourself. Be content to stay the pupil for a while and not try to be the teacher in too many things. You will only over-tax your capabilities and cramp the development of your own gifts.
>
> Above all remember you will find lots of pleasant helpful people thro' life who will always listen and sympathise with your problems, and before whom you don't have to shine and sparkle and be on the top in order to be considered worth-while.

On 23 September Hitler sent an ultimatum demanding the evacuation of German-speaking areas of Czechoslovakia, initially by the 28 September and then by 1 October. Both the British public and the press began to show their disapproval of Chamberlain's policy. By the 26 September Walter noted "the crisis grows" which seems to have prompted his first attendance at a Peace Pledge Union meeting to hear George Lansbury "among others".[13]

However, it also seems likely that his duties at the government department of Directorate of Lands and Accommodation was already involving what might be interpreted as 'war work', surveying properties for the purpose of government requisition in the event of war, and this troubled him greatly. In an undated letter from this period, Mary wrote to him:

> I do hope my reception of your remarks this evening did not appear to you to be more piling on of the agony. I was so horrified I did not dream of trying to comfort you I'm afraid.... I don't know if I feel these things more strongly than you do but it seemed to me the final misery to have to deal with war all day and I was appalled to think that you do so...I do beg of you to do everything in your power to stop yourself 'getting used to it' and to refuse to allow constant association to blunt your sensibilities. There is nothing like constant association with the practical side of slaughter for making us forget the end to which these practical means are leading us. I know your's [sic] is the preventative end of the scale but it is there all the same. I know too so well the circumstances that force you in to this situation and I feel for you so much...
>
> I have just had a letter from Shepperd[14] from Barcelona. He is 50, and tough; he was almost hysterical in parts and says, 'I thought we knew the horror of war 1914-18 but I know now we didn't ever know the beginnings of it.' Bear that in mind all the time my dear and remember every step down the wrong road means treble the effort to come back.

This last paragraph is a reminder that the Spanish Civil War was still in progress and that new and more destructive weapons were being used.

According to the historian C.L. Mowat, "By Tuesday night, September 27, almost everyone in Great Britain expected that the country would be at war next day, or at least by the week-end."[15] One of the greatest fears of the time was of annihilation by aerial bombardment and the government rapidly made provision for air raid shelters and a state of emergency was declared. On 27 September, Walter reported at the office at 9am and was immediately sent north to Lytham St. Anne's with 'Hoctor'—a colleague. Walter's work there was involved with the inspection of properties in Preston. He remarked that St Anne's was an attractive place and 'the name is co-incidental'—perhaps a reference to Anne Parker.

On the 28th Walter wrote that, after waiting all day, good news came that war had been averted and that upon hearing the news, "Hoctor and I shook hands enthusiastically". They went to see the Blackpool illuminations in the evening and he noted that it was "marred by trench digging activity" - another sign that preparations for war were underway. Walter stayed working in the St Anne's office and going in to Blackpool for entertainment in the evening. The fine weather was followed by stormy wet days.

On 1 October Chamberlain returned from his diplomatic talks with Hitler. The Munich Crisis was 'resolved' by France and England refusing to support Czechoslovakia in resisting Hitler, thereby effectively agreeing to his annexation of their Sudetenland territories. This was the agreement that led to Chamberlain's famous declaration of bringing 'peace with honour' and 'peace in our time'. Although there were supposed to be limits and international supervision, Hitler simply took what he wanted of Czechoslovakian lands and began his pogroms against the Jews.

Mary wrote to Walter:

> Was very glad to hear you were at Lytham [St. Anne's] out of this chaos. I did not expect to hear from you as I thought you'd probably be living-in at the office, as most of us seem to be these days, so you can realise how relieved I was to learn of one more of us [the group at Youth House] out of London. You have been much in my thoughts and prayers these last few days when things seemed very black, as it seemed that all the living and suffering you had missed were coming to you in one large burst that might overwhelm you. After last night we all feel so much more optimistic.[16]

She then wrote news of Myra Reilly, wife of Michael, two stalwarts of Youth House, taking her son Nicky down to Somerset and the bliss of being out of London and in the country. Mary was planning to visit Liverpool and hoped that there would be a chance to meet up with Walter for a cup of coffee. She said that she knew Lytham St. Anne's very well because "my husband has relatives there and I've spent many happy days on the coast and the country around." She then mentioned an upcoming lecture by Walter de la Mare, a writer known for his psychological ghost stories, which helps date the letter in relation to others.

A further letter from Mary dated 4 October gives an indication that Walter had been trying to adjust his position at work:

> I was so happy to hear of the sympathetic outlook of your chief and to know that you had been spared so much of the agony of mind I was afraid was coming to you.[17]

She had changed her plans and was not going north after all but would be attending the de la Mare lecture that evening.[18]

Walter returned to London on 4 October and on the Saturday he attended a Youth House dance. More rehearsals and a Hallowe'en party followed. On 17 October 1938 he was elected as a Professional Associate of the Institute of Chartered Surveyors. He had reached professional status as his father had always hoped for him. His social and recreational activities continued unabated, or perhaps even more frenetically, in the face of the approaching war. Rehearsals, hockey matches, dances and dinner dances are spotted through the remaining weeks of the diary and at the end is a note about German language primers presumably because some of his closest new friends were ex-patriate Germans fleeing from fascism. He took a decisive step on 26 November while he was in Blackpool and joined the Peace Pledge Union, signing the pledge:

> War is a crime against humanity. I renounce war, and am therefore determined not to support any kind of war. I am also determined to work

> **THE PEACE PLEDGE UNION**
> "I RENOUNCE WAR AND I WILL NEVER SUPPORT OR SANCTION ANOTHER"
> DICK SHEPPARD HOUSE, 6 ENDSLEIGH STREET, LONDON, WC1   Tel: Euston 5501-2-3
> President: George Lansbury
> Chairman: Stuart Morris
> Hon. Treasurer: Maurice Rowntree
>
> TO ALL WHOM IT MAY CONCERN
>
> I hereby certify that
>
> W.F. Manthorpe
> 1, Warbreck Drive,
> Blackpool.
>
> joined the Peace Pledge Union and signed the above Pledge on 26th November 1938.
>
> Signed .... Chairman.
>
> Sponsors: John Barclay, Harold F. Bing, Vera Brittain, H. Runham Brown, Henry Carter, Mary Gamble, A. Herbert Gray, Laurence Housman, Aldous Huxley, Storm Jameson, George MacLeod, Humphrey Moore, J. Middleton Murry, Max Plowman, Arthur Ponsonby, Charles E. Raven, Bertrand Russell, Alfred Salter, Siegfried Sassoon, Donald Soper, Elizabeth Thorneycroft, Wilfred Wellock, Alex Wood, Arthur Wragg

58. Young Walter's Peace Pledge.

for the removal of all causes of war.

Around the same period, some people were waking up to what was happening to the Jews under the Nazis and in November Bernard Banfield and his wife Elsie, both affiliated to the Quakers, rented a property in Hertfordshire between Drayton Beauchamp and Little Tring called White Houses. It was a pair of old

59. The cottages called White Houses, Tring.

canal worker's cottages which they knocked into one and, with financial help from the Society of Friends, in the autumn of 1938 began taking in refugees from central Europe, mostly Jews.

Elsie Banfield ran the venture as a voluntary warden, supervising the cooking and housework. Years later Bernard recorded that "Many of the refugees were broken psychologically, and racked by anxiety for relations still within Hitler's reach."[19] This endeavour was supported communally by "each member [of Youth House] guaranteeing weekly donations towards the expense"[20] and also doing voluntary work there. The refugees arrived through various organisations—presumably some Quaker—but mostly through Bloomsbury House and many were medical or law students who were shocked at their studies being interrupted.[21]

The year of 1939 opened with Walter starting a new set of evening courses at a polytechnic—French, Maths, Literature, English and Economics (Banking). He seems to have been intent on continuing his education at every opportunity. He was cast in the Curtain Players production of *'Tolstoy'*—the choice presumably because of Tolstoy's pacifist beliefs. He noted Mary's birthday on 10 January. They had dinner and went to see *'3 Smart Girls'*, an American musical comedy movie with Deanna Durban. Two days later he went with Anne to see *'Katie'* and *'Masquerade'*[22] starring Anton Walbrook at the Academy Theatre. He was reading Ernst Toller's *Letters from Prison*[23] and Philip Gibb's *The Cross of Peace*, an anti-war book about France and Germany after World War I. Evidently his mind was very much on the choice he was going to have to face very soon. On Saturday the 14th he bought a new shirt and went for dinner, dancing and a floor show to the Trocadero—an 'exceedingly good evening'. Sunday was spent with Anne and Osmond and Pat[24] (also called Joan) and Ernst and Marguerite, walking on Hampstead Heath and to Kenwood.

The next week he was at a Youth House Committee Meeting and made notes about his poly courses, noting Jones' *Economics of Private Enterprise*. On the Saturday there was a costume dance at Youth House, Anne was absent with a cold but Valerie was "magnificent". On Sunday he went home to Norwich for the day with his Uncle Fred and cousin Margaret. On Wednesday the 25th he went with Anne to a show at the Whitehall which "clearly sets out how that it is impossible to stifle free thought by brute force. But lied about subtle propaganda and a long term policy of gradual extinction of undesirables." On Thursday 26 January he attended a League of Nations rally in Mallet Street near Bedford Square. On the last weekend of the month he was skating at Wembley with Jessica (Grimm) and Ralph (Swingler) and attending a Curtain Players social. The next day he was invited to tea by Ernst and Anne, who both shared a birthday on 29 January. The party comprised Anne, Ernst, Mary and Margaret.

In February he went to see *The Citadel* with Robert Donat and Ralph Richardson, a film based on the novel by A.J. Cronin about the issues of working-class health and the medical establishment. Later in the month he went with two Norwich friends to visit 'John's Studio with dinner at the Candy Shop'. This would have been John Gregory[25] whom Walter had known at the Maddermarket Theatre in Norwich and had been working as a personal assistant to Edward 'Ted' Seago, the Norfolk landscape painter. Walter wrote that he viewed Ted's pictures, which had recently been shown in New York at the Carrol Carstairs Gallery. Walter was "pleased to find that John is a pacifist."[26]

His diary continued with notes of films, theatre, committee meetings, playing in hockey matches. On 10 February he attended a Peace Pledge Union Meeting. On Saturday night he was at the Rendezvous restaurant on Wardour Street with Ernst, Reg and Osmond Leslie, "an excellent dinner for 4 shillings with wine". They went for coffee and cake to the Troika and beer at the Regent's Palace Lounge. He obviously enjoyed London life. Sunday was spent having lunch with Anne at Maidenhead and walking via the Marlows to join the ramblers [from YH] for tea at Henley. He spent an afternoon and evening with Mary, went to a twenty first birthday party and John lent him his car for the return journey. He continued rehearsing, went to see Auden and Isherwood's *The Ascent of F6* [27] at the Tavistock Theatre, lunched at the Regent's Palace with Ernst and Osmond, walked through the park and had tea at the Waldorf, and participated in discussion groups. At the annual Chartered Surveyors Institute Dance, at Gresham House, the principal guests were the Marquis of Reading and Sir Thomas Inskip. The latter was Minister for the Co-ordination of Defence 1939-40[28] although not perceived at the time to be very effective. Walter met up with professional colleagues from Norwich.

The busy-ness of his diary implies that Walter was energetically pursuing all the enjoyable possibilities that were open to him while still keeping a wary eye on the darkening political horizon.

Notes

1. WFM Diary for 1938.
2. Surname unknown.
3. Titmuss became a member of the Board in 1937 and did much to sort out their financial affairs.
4. Oakley, p.72.
5. Paper by Bernard Banfield, March 1987.
6. Krishnamurti was raised by Theosophists to become a new World Teacher but later developed his own style of spiritual teachings.
7. see Appendix I—List of members.
8. After the war Haynes Dixon moved to the Central Office of Information and later still married the novelist Rumer Godden. See Chisholm, Anne. *Rumer Godden*, 1999, pp. 205-6.
9. Ernest Hammond had fled from Germany. He and his Swiss wife Marguerite became lifelong friends of Walter and Anne.
10. Mowat, p. 608.
11. Ibid.
12. Presumably Morley College—a leading adult education centre on Westminster Bridge Road.
13. George Lansbury (1859–1940) was a British politician, pacifist and social reformer who led the Labour Party from 1932 to 1935.
14. Unknown person—not Dick Sheppard.
15. Mowat, p.615
16. Letter from Mary, 1/2/3 October 1938. In possession of the author.
17. Undated letter from Mary, enveloped franked October 4 1938. In possession of the author.
18. Ibid.
19. From a paper written by Bernard Banfield, March 1987.
20. From an account of Youth House written by Anne Manthorpe (née Parker). In the possession of the author.
21. Bloomsbury House—part of London University.
22. A play by Lermontov set in St Petersburg with an Othello-like plot.
23. Toller was a playwright and left-wing revolutionary who had been imprisoned for five years for his resistance in Bavaria to the central government in Berlin. He was exiled from Germany in 1933 and this book was published in 1936.
24. Osmond and Joan Leslie, as they became when they married.
25. 1914-1996, born in Norwich, a leading dancer, choreographer and teacher, as well as the author of many books on ballet.

26. According to his obituary in the *Independent* (31 October 1996 by Gregor Koenig), John Gregory embraced conscientious objection and toured with the Carl Rosa ballet under a Russian stage name, but later was 'forced into uniform' and toured with ENSA.
27. First published in 1936.
28. Sir Thomas Inskip, 1876–1947. After the war he was accused by some of failure to rearm.

9. March 1939—New Year 1940

In the months after Munich Britain seriously began to re-arm. In particular the Royal Air Force was expanded and the Territorial Army brought up to strength in preparation for a British expeditionary force. Anti-aircraft guns and modern planes were under production and radar stations were being built. In mid-March of 1939 Germany invaded the Czech provinces of Bohemia and Moravia and began to make aggressive gestures towards Poland. Chamberlain announced that, in the event of any real threat, Britain would have to support them and the government signed a reciprocal agreement with the Polish government.

Walter's film and theatre going continued. He took in a production of J. M Synge's celebration of the Irish language *Playboy of the Western World* which he thought superb, "beautifully acted and produced". He and Anne saw what has become something of a cult homoerotic German film, *Mädchen in Uniform* with an all-female cast at the Classic cinema. Walter noted that it had "intense acting". Then, still in March "Mary dropped a bombshell in various directions that she is leaving the group", which since she was a leading advocate of pacifism and a support to her younger friends must have hit them hard. By now the lines were being drawn in the sand and Walter attended a Queen's Hall Meeting on 18 March in Support of National Petition for a New Peace Conference.

A few days later he went with Mary to see *These Foolish Things*, a revue show with 'Mayfair' songs at the Palladium which must have been in stark contrast to the Youth House production *Tolstoy* which the players finally performed on 29 and 30 March. Before he went home for Easter Walter found time to hear the great Italian tenor Gigli at the Albert Hall and on 4 April he was "Deposed from Position of Social Secretary at House Meeting". It's unclear what this meant to him—or why it happened. Either his own social life was too busy or he had more serious matters on his mind, or a bit of both. Back in Norfolk he spent his time sailing with friends and his brother Jack on the Broads. He returned to London on 13 April "after a wonderful and much needed holiday" and went to *The Great Waltz*, an American biopic of Richard Strauss II, with Anne in the evening.

The next day he found the "Office Awful", quite possibly because he was doing war work. But he had saved the means to buy a car and picked it up from Enfield. On Saturday 15 April he had dinner with Reg, Osmond and Ernst—the usual Saturday night men's group—at *The Chanticleer*. The following day he was at a *thé dansant*. The close-knit group at Youth House seemed to be breaking up; at a meeting on the 18th, Jessica Grimm, one of the staff members, informed them that she was leaving, as was another member called Beatrice.

Walter was reading *Power: A New Social Analysis* by Bertrand Russell which was a polemic about how political enlightenment and human understanding could lead to peace, and also *Why War* by C.M. Joad, the popular philosopher, arguing that war was not inevitable and could be avoided. Walter had a whole set of Joad's books.

Thursday 20 April he went to the Westminster theatre at John Gregory's invitation to see T.S. Elliot's *Family Reunion*. John was working as an understudy. "Excellent show only lacking in movement. Michael Redgrave and Katherine [sic] Lacey."[1] Lunches at the Strand Palace, theatre visits, squash, new rehearsals and time with Anne fill Walter's diary. Then, rather typically, he branched out to learn about something completely new. He drove down to Portsmouth and took an airplane to Ryde on the Isle of Wight, where he walked in the rain and then returned to London the same day. He noted, "My first flight a magnificent sensation. Car ran marvellously."

Significantly for all the pacifists at Youth House, at the end of April 1939, the government introduced a Military Training Bill that provided for six months compulsory military training for 20–21 year-olds. Most importantly, even at this early stage of what was essentially preparation for conscription, the Bill included provision that individual conscience was to respected. As in the previous war, conscientious objection was to be verified by Tribunals (of 5 men) but the penalization of conscience was now recognised as both wrong and ineffective; tribunals were to recommend suitable civil work and the possibility of 'cat-and-mouse' incarceration was deflected if not entirely eliminated. Effectively, the 1,500 Absolutists of World War I together with the approximate 14,500 Alternativists, who had survived years of prison and hard labour had won a victory in terms of a public and parliamentary shift in consciousness with regard to the rights of the individual in a civilized society.[2] But the passing of the Bill certainly heralded the end of peace, if not the start of war.

On 5 May, Walter attended a meeting of the Peace Pledge Union where Hans Arnold spoke about the Bruderhof—Christian communities characterised by non-violence, peace-making and common ownership. Presumably to help with the refugee project he drove Anne and Pat down to Tring in Hertfordshire where they stayed overnight. They came back the next day stopping for tea at Whipsnade. In the evening he went to or heard *The Village Wooing* ("very good") and later *Fumed Oak* (only "fair").

There was a new Curtain Players production of *Alice in Wonderland* in the pipeline and Walter was cast as the March Hare, which seems a rather unlikely part for him. On Friday 12 May he attended the Peace Pledge Union AGM and began to attend their meetings on an almost weekly basis. He noted in his diary that a planned 'mock tribunal' to be held on 22 May at Caxton Hall was cancelled but this was evidence that the pacifists were getting ready for the confrontations ahead.

Friday 26 May he went on a Youth House camping holiday starting at Henley with Anne, Pat and Osmond Leslie for several days including boating. Although Hitler was now ramping up his aggressive rhetoric, "The spring and summer [of 1939] were a time of waiting. Some people were tense, others banished thought with a forced and hectic gaiety, having a last fling on a holiday abroad or in some still unfenced seaside spot; almost all were resigned."[3] Walter seems to have been doing both: tensely attending to pacifist activities and enjoying every last minute of peace.

In early July, rather incredibly just two months before war was declared, he and Anne and Ruth (Parry?) and John (Wroughton?) embarked on a trip to Germany. It is not clear whether this had been long-planned or was one last attempt at building relationships between nations or simply a chance to see what was really going on. They left on Saturday the 8th from Victoria Station and arrived at Ostend at 8.30am had meal at Hotel Maritime and then took the 11.00 train for Köln.

His diary entries recounted the bare bones of the trip:

> Arrived Köln 6 or thereabouts. Met Paul and had breakfast there. Saw Daisy off on train to Dresden. Did circular tour of Köln on the tram and caught

60. Women members in the garden at Youth House. Back row (from left): Winifred Shields (later Swingler), Joan Tremelis. Front row (from left): Joan Miller, Jessica Grimm, Diana Geiger.

61. Walter's Peace Pledge Union lapel badge.

train 10.20 to Oberwesel via Koblenz and Bad Emms. Met by Herr Saar and escorted to Hotel Gertum [?] for lunch. — then slept until 6 after which dinner reading and bed.'

Monday 10 July

Weather warm but showery. Oberwesel [a town south of Koblenz on the Rhine where they stayed for most of the holiday] is small (5000 inhabs) and quiet in the wine growing district with steep sides of the valley all around. After a late breakfast and lunch we off to St Goar a rather more spacious township not a long walk by road following the river and returning by steamer (40f). It is now cold and dull.

He then made mention of the prevalence of uniformed soldiers everywhere but still said that his impression was "no war". They visited a schloss, possibly Schönburg, and a local beer cellar in the evening. Tuesday was spent walking in the hills enjoying views of the Rhine valley. On Wednesday he and Anne walked upriver to Kant, crossed the river by ferry and walked back on the opposite side to Oberwesel.

Thursday he spent making sketches in the morning and took a ferry to Lorelei St Goar (a rocky cliff) where there was a fine open-air theatre. In the evening he was drinking with soldiers and SS men—no doubt still trying to gauge the way the wind was blowing.

On the Friday John slipped and sprained his ankle. Walter and Anne did more walking in the hills and came back from St Goar by boat. "Another good evening drinking with Erich Schwann and his frau". On the Sunday they moved on to Frankfurt and then via Mannheim to Gernsbach. "Film show in hotel in evening including photographs of the German forces in Spain." On Monday there was swimming and a visit to Schloss Eberstein. On Tuesday more swimming and walks in the forests. John seems to have recovered. On Wednesday they made a steep climb to Tenfelsmühle over 800 metres. It was hot and sultry and they found an inn for lunch and were then caught in a thunder storm during the descent—"soaked to the skin." They enjoyed drinks at the *Wilden Mann*. Thursday was spent at Mummelsee and Friday at Baden Baden before they began the long train journey home arriving on Sunday 23 July at Victoria where Ernst and Pat met them.

Another holiday followed in early August when he went walking and Youth Hostelling with Anne, Osmond and Pat at Maidenhead, staying at Boulton Lock. Sunday 6 August was a glorious day and they walked upriver to Bourne End with lunch, punting. He went home to Norwich on 12 August and Anne saw him off at Liverpool St Station after a lunch at the Strand Palace. In the evening he went out to Horning to book a boat called 'Mischief' for a few days.

The next day he was sailing with Jack from Horning to Thurne Mouth and back to Ludham Bridge. There was a fair wind and the boat handled magnificently. The day after they sailed again up to Neatishead Staithe and then across Barton broad to Stalham. On Tuesday there as still no wind and they reached Barton. They had difficulty getting through the Shoal, then there was excellent sailing and a stiff breeze to Horning. "Mischief beats everything."

On Wednesday he went with his father to Wroxham "Quanting all day. [that is punting] Not a breath of wind even on the Broad but marvellous weather". On the Thursday he sailed with Geoff Crane at Wroxham Broad and had "a fine swim in Salhouse Broad. Arrived at Horning during finish of regatta and beat the field."

62. Anne Parker and Walter Manthorpe in Germany July 1939.

Meanwhile Hitler was preparing to invade Poland. On 24 August the British Parliament was recalled to enact an Emergency Powers Bill. For several days attempts were made at diplomatic negotiation. When Walter got back to work on 25 August he was sent up north again to the office in Lytham St. Anne's. Sunday was spent in the office, and in the afternoon or evening he went to Blackpool with Philip Price[4] and another colleague named Reeves. Ever restless and physically active, he walked home from Blackpool, went riding on the beach on Tuesday and swimming on Wednesday. By 29 August it was clear that Germany's terms were close to an ultimatum and that Britain and France were no longer willing to back down. On Sunday 3 September 1939 England declared war on Germany and in the afternoon a National Forces (Armed Services) Bill was enacted. Conscription was back in full force.

Walter had been writing to Mary about his concerns for the future—in particular about whether he should marry Anne and whether they should move to Ireland— the latter an option he had already raised with his father. Mary wrote a long letter back starting with her shock at the declaration of war:

> I had supreme faith that this would not happen. I was utterly and
> absolutely sure that humanity would not allow politicians to lead us

into slaughtering each other. I was in charge of our office on the Sunday morning. I had only juniors of 16 and boy messengers. We were not informed that war was declared and my first intimation was the air-raid warning.[5] You can imagine how I felt being responsible for the safety of these youngsters in a nice target like the three railway stations [perhaps a location near Paddington, King's Cross and Euston]. ... Every one said how did you keep so calm. No one realised I was paralized!![6]

She took some comfort in that there were no signs of jingoism or people thinking the war was heroic [as they had done in World War I] and that people didn't hate the Germans. With regard to Walter and Anne, she wrote, "I wondered when I saw your letter if it was to say you were married and rather murmured a prayer that it would not be so." She counselled him to wait, to live together if that was a solution to their being together—Anne was still in London—that marriage was too permanent a step and might spoil both their lives. She felt that if he felt it necessary to ask her advice then he wasn't sure enough to take the step. As far as his idea of moving to Ireland, she strongly discouraged him. She had sympathy for his disgust at the political state of Europe and had even decided to leave herself when the war was over and go to New Zealand or Canada—but, as pacifists, she felt they must stay and see out the war and bear it with everyone else. "Believe me you would not have a moment's happiness. How do you feel now to know that your friends are in London, struggling round in the dark carrying gas masks and always prepared to duck and run—do you think you'd find peace of mind in Ireland?" Mary still had great faith in pacifism, "the brotherhood is there, it's only that we haven't yet learnt to put it in to practice."

She recalled with pleasure the many lectures they had attended together and the occasions of their discussions while walking over Westminster Bridge, "sometimes in the fog sometimes in the moonlight but always with some measure of peace and all the wars cannot take those from us."[7]

During the period from October 1939 until May 1940, known now as The Phoney War, Britain waited for a German military offensive that the under-mechanised Nazis were unable to deliver. In anticipation of aerial bombardment, the British government took some drastic measures on the domestic front including The Blackout, which resulted in a steady number of casualties and deaths from car accidents, and the evacuation of young children from London to the countryside thus breaking up families and causing distress and, in many cases, trauma. A high proportion of the children returned to London within months - in time for the Blitz.

On 1 October 1939 there was a Call-up Proclamation, all men aged 20-21 who had not already done so had apply for registration with the military authorities. Walter was 23 coming up to 24 and carried on much as usual in the atmosphere of tense anticipation. He visited Youth House for a dance on 7 October and then went home to Norwich for a few days. Back in London he had lunch and dinner with his friends Ernst, Osmond, Marguerite, Pat and Anne at the Brasserie Universelle, a modest but lively-looking restaurant in Piccadilly. He visited the peace Pledge Union HQ on 12 October and then returned to work at Lytham St. Anne's. Anne saw him off at Euston Station.

He had also met up with Mary because she wrote to him in November 1939 about the fact that they had not been able to get on the same comfortable wavelength that they had used to have.

> I feel there is so much we <u>ought</u> to say to each other and we don't because time presses so and we cannot settle comfortably into our usual relationship.
>
> After seeing you in October I knew afterwards that there was so much I should have said about the dangers of young bachelor friends in unconsummated marriages. This time I felt there was even more I should have said in reply to your observation that you were realising the irrevocable step matrimony is. However, it will all have to wait because you know by now that I can never approach these things unless specifically asked to do so. I always feel otherwise it's an impertinence, so now I must wait for another opportunity.[8]

Mary went on to describe an evening spent at a WEA class on psychology at which the questions and conversation turned only to war. She envied Walter having stimulating social contacts.

> You know I always wanted you to get away from Y.H. because I felt it had served its purpose in your life. It served you at an age when one does things in crowds because one has not yet sufficient social confidence to do otherwise. It is a <u>good</u> manifestation of the gang spirit. It seems it's going a little too far now as matrimony is its latest craze. I saw Elfreda in the week

63. Brasserie Universalle, Piccadilly Circus. Postcard

and was almost horrified at her news of marriage all over the place. When something is 'the thing' they all do it.

She had also attended a talk by Barbara Wootton, an economist, conscientious objector and promoter of a Federal Union of European countries. The meeting was at the Trade Union Club and Mary was frustrated at the low standard of intelligence amongst the rest of the audiences who were all anti-capitalist. This seems to be a confirmation that many of the Youth House pacifists were far from being socialists, then or later. The occasion made her despair of the value of adult education. She asked Walter to let her know where he is going to be for Christmas as they might be able to meet up if she were to be in Liverpool. In a December letter she thanked him for a gift of flowers and sent a short letter to say that she was extremely busy at work with the Christmas post and might be going to Ireland for the holiday.

Then, after all the months of intellectual speculation and frenetic activity, the implications of war began to close in. At some point in December 1939 Walter was seen leaving a PPU meeting in Lytham St. Anne's and this was reported to the Town Clerk. Without any explanation he was removed from his current position and transferred to the Blackpool office. Later, when the situation became more critical, Walter was to write:

> The circumstances surrounding my removal from St Annes are still to me largely unknown, apart from the fact that some person had become aware of my opinions and because of this it was considered advisable that I should be transferred to Blackpool. I was engaged in no activities in St. Annes and although I have friends there with whom discussion naturally took place I could not remember having ostentatiously and indiscreetly publicised my views. However, it appears to me that the position was brought to the notice of the Town Clerk of St Annes and at an interview with the Director of Lands and Accommodation it was understood that I would in future take every precaution to prevent my private life of ideas conflicting with my official duties. There was no question of any activities and my impression of the matter was that an inopportune remark had, in a small town, been seized upon at a time when the actions of the Department were not being received in a favourable manner. [presumably requisitioning property for government use] I would, however, emphasise the fact that my relationships both with the members of the profession whom I met officially and with a circle of personal friends were of an extremely amicable nature. In particular I should perhaps mention that I stayed for a considerable period at the home of the secretary of the St. Anne's hotel owners' Association and that my strong friendship with the family continues unbroken.[9]

There were two issues emerging at this time. One was the interpretation of the role of the Peace Pledge Union: was it political or philosophical? Secondly, for those who considered it a political force in opposition to the current government, there was a move to eradicate it or at least curtail its activities.

On 10 January 1940 Mary wrote a long letter to Walter, now living at 1 Warbeck Drive, North Shore Blackpool, wishing him 'everything good' for the New Year. First she responded to Walter's comments on "batchelors [sic] in unconsummated marriages" which referred to the situation faced by homosexual men at a time when the practice was illegal. Homosexual men married for domestic and social convenience, sometimes to lesbians or to compliant or even unsuspecting women, Siegfried Sassoon is a famous example. It is not quite clear what the implications were amongst their Youth House friends, but it was evidently an acknowledged and concerning issue. Continuing with Youth House gossip, someone had embarrassed Walter by making a remark about Mary "taking something belonging to Anne!!" as though Walter was involved romantically with Mary, which, although they were close, does not seem to have been the case. Mary also mentioned Anne showing "her subconscious guilt in experiencing a thrill to which she knows she is not entitled" which may refer to having sex before marriage, or something else entirely. She also adds a warning: "And also an excellent example of dangers of the relationship which I tried to tell you!!" indicating again her opposition to Walter getting too deeply involved with Anne.

> I thought your argument for marriage excellent but still don't agree with you. I know all you feel you have in common but it means very little really. Some of the happiest marriages have few tastes in common. Happy marriage is based on a fundamental sweetness of character that will allow for all those differences and never ask for them to be changed.
>
> One thing I must say Marriage is _not_ inevitable and from my observation of your character I think it very probable that you are one of those who could find much fulfilment in life, single. Why do you think marriage inevitable?

She then described her few days holiday in an hotel in Ireland with friends which was very festive with bridge and games and charades. On Boxing Day she had attended the meet of the local hunt (as had Walter where he was) and a dance in the evening that went on into the small hours and she mentions a slight flirtation she was having. She thought of Walter often because he would have 'adored being there' with lovely countryside and being outdoors all day, together with the sophisticated and "hilarious fun and drink"'. This confirms Walter's aspirational tastes for the good-life.

The next section of the letter is about a long-standing discussion between them about the sublimation of the sexual instinct. Without friends around and in the black out in London Mary had few diversions to turn to. Previously she had sublimated her desires into drama and advising her young friends. Now she found herself "taking far more notice of males in general and getting more satisfaction out of kisses and caresses (Ireland)." She was concerned that sex was taking up too prominent a place her life which she did not like. Mary seems to have been either a Roman Catholic or High Anglican, most probably the latter since she was soon-to-be divorced. She then went on to discuss a man she was currently involved with and may even marry. She added at the end a comment on her romantic involvements, "The sexual interest does not apply to you, so I won't be causing you any embarrassment."

Notes

1. The play was first performed on 21 March 1939 at the Westminster Theatre, London, with Michael Redgrave as Harry, Helen Haye as Lady Monchensey and Catherine Lacey as Agatha. It ran until 22 April 1939.
2. See Fenner Brockway's Introduction and Chapter 1 in Hayes,D. *Challenge of Conscience: The Story Of The Conscientious Objectors of 1939-1945*, 1949.
3. Mowat, p.641.
4. Philip and Marjorie Price.
5. A false alarm—what followed were the months of the so-called Phoney War.
6. Letter from Mary, September 1939. In the possession of the author.
7. Letter from Mary. In possession of the author.
8. Letter undated but envelope is franked 28 November 1939.
9. From his 17 May 1940 letter to the Establishment Officer, Mr Spencer, see Appendix 5.

10. January 1940—July 1940

As the Youth House entanglements and romantic dilemmas jittered on, the war machine was catching up with Walter. In January 1940 he received his call up notice. Unfortunately for him there was now a nationwide reaction to COs particularly in County Councils who wanted to dismiss or not employ pacifists.[1] In Blackpool in 1940 this wave of antipathy manifested itself in an Anti-Conscientious Objector League. Not only was Walter typical of the new kind of CO—educated, humanitarian, internationalist and horrified at the thought of another war in Europe—but as a civil servant he was at the heart of the storm of public and official abhorrence.[2]

There were many more COs coming forward than there had been in World War I[3] and the call-up was administered by The Ministry of Labour and National Service, unlike the First World War when it came under the War Office. This signalled a major change in the policy of the government. Prime Minister Chamberlain had been quite clear that conscientious objection would again be respected. However, the government was not going to risk making martyrs this time round—not least because it had many more men to deal with—over 60,000 registered COs. There were three possibilities for applicants: unconditional exemption, alternative non-combatant work in the army, or civilian work in acceptable occupations such as ambulance driving and farm work. Only 3,000 were given unconditional exemption and most were absorbed into non-combatant or civilian work. As in World War I the absolutists who refused any co-operation at all with the state were imprisoned, usually for short periods but sometimes repeatedly and they suffered both from the system and their fellow prisoners.[4]

Registration took place at local Employment Exchanges on a Saturday and COs had to announce their status and fill in a separate form, sometimes at a separate counter. It took some courage in front of willing recruits but there was very little reported abuse or discrimination at this stage.[5] COs had to give their name, address, marital status, and their parents' occupation. They were then given a form to fill in describing exactly what they objected to, whether it be being registered for military service, performing military services or performing combatant duties. They could express whether they were looking for absolute exemption or were willing to support the war effort in civilian or non-combatant work and supply a personal statement to be completed within 14 days. The PPU's *Peace News* gave regular advice to those going to register and there was advice and support from the Central Board of Conscientious Objectors which had been formed in 1939 to lobby parliament, monitor legislation, keep archives and set up employment agencies.[6] It, too, published a journal, called *Bulletin*.

The die was cast and Walter began preparing his Statement: the essential document for the inevitable Tribunal.[7] He sent the hand-written draft to his father for his comments. His father's letter of response shows that he himself was still guided by a firm religious faith and had some difficulty in following his son's viewpoint on the issue. He replied at the end of January saying, "My reactions are that you have followed your individual reasoning and not simply quoted stereotyped objections which is all to the good, you have also steered clear of religious consideration that might have arisen if you were questioned, although I myself could not exactly follow your line of reasoning." He added that although distance made it impossible to lend him support, he considered that Walter would be all the stronger for having to work out his position on his own and would have the support of "thousands of Prophets and martyrs" who were always there, "when you follow what you believe to be right."[8] He continued in a religious vein: "I feel honoured to be able to help you to state your belief in what has been the strength of man since the Creation and will be till the new world becomes real." And made some suggested amendments to the document which have not survived.

He added some family news that "Jack finished at Howes[9] on Saturday last and is looking out for another post. Hope you are taking care and bearing mind that we talk and think about you that this little family circle of arcs is one of which you are always part of."

Walter asked for supporting letters from his father and from Arthur Eddington[10] which would seem to indicate that either he hadn't made any strong contacts in the PPU, or that he felt the family circle would be his strongest line of defence. Eddington's testimony has not survived, but his father's letter supports an unbroken line of pacifism from World War I:

> ... He was born during the stress of the last War I his father determined then that War was futile, that came what would there would be no compromise with it and in that atmosphere the consciousness of our family has developed against War. My association with the

64. Jack Manthorpe aged about 18.

65. *Jack with some of his friends third from right, Peggy Cann, second from right and Mel Cann second from left.*

conscientious objectors of the last War continued unbroken with them including George Lansbury and the late Canon Dick Sheppard, and my active membership of both the No More War Movement and the Peace Pledge union testify to the environment of the whole life of W F Manthorpe. The State has recognised the freedom of conscience as an essential part of its Constitution and we who hold to this principle believe it to be the corner stone of the future edifice of civilisation. Believing in the Brotherhood of man and the Fatherhood of God and the inevitability of Death to those that take the sword either actually or by proxy I would understandingly support the testimony submitted by W F Manthorpe.

On 15 February Mary wrote again thanking Walter for a recent letter which perhaps included details of his Statement, "Candidly you amazed me, I had not realized how much you had grown up." She wrote to tell him that she would be thinking of him on Saturday, presumably when he registered and counselled him not to be dramatic but to "remember your own pleas for simplicity, simplicity, simplicity." She was concerned for his poor mother having to go through this ordeal again. She added some encouraging news of friends who had joined the PPU and finished by advising him to "Keep your heart high my sweet, and send me a line as to how you fare."

On 22 February a question was asked in the House of Commons[11] about the activities of the Peace Pledge Union with their presence at Employment Exchanges being described by Sir William Davison[12] as "subversive" and in effect "picketing" and an abuse of their freedom to opinion. The Secretary of State,

Sir John Anderson, replied that their activities were being closely watched and "the question of whether special measures are called for will be kept in view". In response Labour MP Reginald Sorenson[13] asked whether the Christian churches were to be regarded as "subversive".

Walter's statement of objection, dated 27 February 1940, was based on two convictions:

> a)   My belief that humanity is intrinsically a unity and that one man is no different from another—different in that he is not also a member of humanity.
>
> b)   My belief that the intrinsic unity is inviolable.

While he recognised that he was part of the political state, he believed he had a higher allegiance to the human race. He emphasised his rigorous moral upbringing and while acknowledging the threat of Nazi ideas and the need for sacrifice (a hark back to World War I), he was not convinced that killing was the answer since "war is itself an expression of that violence, hatred and corruption that it seeks to eradicate". In other words, he repudiated the idea of a 'just' war and instead offered Huxley's argument that the ends cannot justify the means. He then outlined his life in a multi-national community (Youth House) and his involvement in their humanitarian activities, as well as his performance in moral dramas. More recently his involvement with the Peace Pledge Union had included becoming joint secretary in Blackpool, leading "a series of discussions on the essential philosophy of pacifism, and contributing to funds to help pacifists rendered workless."[14]

On 20 April Mary wrote another long letter, once again expressing her anxiety about Walter's relationship with Anne: "First of all I am so glad you are not rushing into matrimony and secondly I am most anxious to hear if you have any news of the tribunal yet." Mary herself was newly single and explains:

> After all the alarms and excursions my divorce has gone through at last and on Sept 15 (D.V.) [deo volente] I shall be legally a free woman. I am not going to marry Leslie. It is much too involved to begin to explain here I must wait till I see you. Of course I miss him desperately. That preciousness and importance to someone leaves a ghastly loneliness in its wake. No wonder people will hang on to any one sooner than be alone.

She went on to give him news of a Youth House revue and of various films and plays she had seen and ended with a recommendation to read: "*Grapes of Wrath* by John Steinbeck (the man who wrote '*Of Mice and Men*). If you haven't beg borrow or steel [sic] it and read it …….. It shows good decent kindly intentioned simple people – and the way the moneyed scum make puppets of them." Mary signed off: "I still think of you with the same affection and interest – but I'm incoherent with tiredness. Bless you. Mary."

66. *The Shire Hall, Lancaster Castle. Postcard.*

A few days later, Walter faced the tribunal. There were twelve regional tribunals held in county courts, chaired by a county court judge, and with four members on the panel which had to include a trade unionist, a significant improvement on World War I. Their only task was to deal with exemptions—again a great improvement.[15] There was no military representative and there was the opportunity to appeal. The job of the panel was simply, but not easily, to assess the CO's sincerity with regard to conscience, either on religious, political or moral grounds. Walter's tribunal was held on Thursday 25 April at the Shire Hall in Lancaster Castle. He had asked for complete exemption from National Service "since I must completely reject the principle of the law of compulsion for war purposes." He also asked for the tribunal to be held in camera because he was a civil servant and this was granted. Unfortunately, this attracted particular attention to his case.

The *West Lancashire Evening Gazette* reported on the same day:

> On the grounds that his employment and the department in which he was engaged might be adversely affected by the publicity, the application of Walter Frederick Manthorpe, a 23-year-old civil servant of Warbreek-drive,[sic] Blackpool, joint secretary of the Blackpool Peace Pledge Union, that his case should be heard in camera, was granted by the tribunal for conscientious objectors at Lancaster today.

It also reported the outcome of the case:

> Application was registered on condition that he undertook first-aid or A.R.P. work of a civil character, under civilian control.[16]

So, Walter had his exemption from military service but only on condition that he do work of national importance. Unfortunately, the matter didn't end there. Walter's case quickly blew up into a local scandal. The next day, 26 April, the *West Lancashire Evening Gazette* followed up with a story titled *Conchie" Case Heard in Camera* about the reactions from the Town Clerk of Lytham St. Anne's, Mr Walter Heap, the man who had reported Walter's PPU activities earlier in the year, who said:

> I can only say that I was amazed when I saw in "The Evening Gazette" last night that a civil servant, well known in this town for his peace propaganda activities, had been exempted military service on condition that he look for first-aid or A.R.P. work after his case had been heard in private.
>
> I have no personal feelings against a conscientious objector as such but I take strong objection to conscientious objector who insists upon spreading his deplorable propaganda amongst other people.
>
> I cannot understand,' continued Mr Heep, 'why anyone applying for exemption as a conscientious objector should seek to be heard in private.
>
> If he has a conscientious objection to serving his country, there does not appear to be any reason at all why he should not have the courage of his convictions.
>
> Neither can I understand how anyone can seriously claim to have a conscientious objection to serve his country and at the same time accept a salary from the very Government which is prosecuting the war with all the means at its disposal.
>
> The two views seem to be illogical and inconsistent.
>
> I had three patriotic youths on my staff who had been studying very hard for long periods with a view to taking professional examinations.
>
> They had to go. Their careers were cut short and they are now receiving 2s a day. Their cases could be multiplied by hundreds'.[17]

The Gazette also interviewed Ald. W. Hope, Chairman of Lytham St. Anne's Council Rating and Valuation Committee who "earnestly supported the Town Clerk's opinion" and said he would move a resolution at the monthly Council meeting on Monday:

> That in the opinion of this Council that conscientious objectors should be compelled to carry out work of national importance at rates of pay no higher, and under conditions no better than, those of H.M Forces.

He added: "In result of the case heard in camera at Lancaster, one would think that Sir John Anderson [the Home Secretary] would take action."

Not content with pursuing the story via local officials, in the same issue the *Gazette* editorialised on the story:

Secrecy for "Conchie"
Why?

> On the grounds that his employment and the Government department in which he was engaged might be adversely affected by the publicity, the application of a 23-year-old civil servant described as joint secretary of the Blackpool Peace Pledge Union, that his case should be heard in camera was granted by Lancaster Tribunal for conscientious objectors.
>
> The applicant was registered as a conscientious objector on condition that he undertook first aid or A.R.P. work of a civil character under civilian control.
>
> The public will want to know why a civil servant should be treated any differently from anyone else in this matter. They will also want to know why it should be necessary to hear his case in secret to avoid adversely affecting his employment.
>
> How can a civil servant conscientiously take money from any Government to the war policy of which he is openly opposed on grounds of his conscience?
>
> Doesn't his conscience revolt from such a course? How can he be a loyal and conscientious servant of a State at war if he conscientiously objects to that war? Especially when he joins an organisation openly opposed to the Government?
>
> These are questions which need answering and quickly. The A.R.P. unit which he joins will probably invite an answer.
>
> The earnest and patriotic spirit of the first-aid and A.R.P. services is such that members will probably take a keen personal interest in whether civil service "conchies" should be dumped on them after a secret hearing.[18]

Having seen the press coverage, a Mr Lingard of the Blackpool Peace Pledge Union wrote to Walter:

> I am very sorry for your sake, to notice the way the opposition are going for you on account of your alleged pacifist propaganda activities. Were it not that the press (thoroughly 'Hitlerized' in Blackpool) is able to influence Public Opinion so erroneously — and the possibility of your own personal career being affected, the pother would be somewhat amusing.[19]

He went on to say that he had not associated Walter with "the active element in the PPU" and had thought of him as a casual sympathiser although he had wished he *would* get more involved.

I am astonished to find that as a Civil Servant you are presumed by intelligent Conservatives to have sold body, mind and spirit to the State. Surely your contract for service does not imply such! ...

Lingard felt that the attacks in the press "regarding your and other cases being heard privately shows up their ignorance of the law – if not their contempt for it". He offered any help he could give and suggested that Walter might get in touch with the Council for Civil Liberties.

Walter evidently got on the case immediately and asked the former Blackpool secretary, Reginald Baxter, of the PPU to give him a letter saying exactly what his involvement had been. In a letter of 26 April Baxter confirmed that Walter had been joint-secretary for a period six weeks only and that, "Never at any time during his connection with this Group has he been concerned with the dissemination of pacifist propaganda, so far as I am aware. Furthermore, Although invited and even pressed to speak at Pacifist Public Meetings in Blackpool and in another town, he did, on both occasions, decline to take part." Walter had opened some discussions on philosophy at the Blackpool Meeting House of the Society of Friends but "In all conversations at which I have been present, and in his conversation generally with the group, Mr. Manthorpe has preserved the utmost discretion, to such effect that only a small circle of acquaintances were even aware of his vocation; nor has he ever impressed me as being a person who would ostentatiously try to persuade his views upon others."[20]

It was this letter that Walter forwarded later to Mr Spencer at the Department of Works.

On 27 April *The West Lancashire Evening Gazette* continued its campaign against conscientious objectors. The previous evening there had been a meeting of the Blackpool Women's Unionist Association at the Conservative Club in Blackpool and it had been attended by the local MP Mr J. Roland Robinson. *The Gazette* enthusiastically reported on the views of his views:

'Work on the Land for 'Conchie groups'

Blackpool M.P.'s Plan

'Make them Produce Food'

'And Pay then Same Rates as Soldiers'

I am strongly in favour of forming conscientious objectors groups. I would put these men to work on the land. I would make them produce the food which they are eating, and I would pay them the rates of pay which are paid to soldiers. Make them work hard on the land. There would be nothing offensive to their consciences in that."

Loud and prolonger applause greeted this passage in a speech by Mr J.

Roland Robinson, M.P., at the annual meeting of the Blackpool Women's Unionist Association yesterday, in the course of which he sternly attacked men whom he called the 'black sheep of the Civil Service'—conscientious objectors who refuse to fight for the State in its hour of crisis.

I most strongly object to the type of man who is prepared to accept the government's money by day and sabotages the government's war efforts in the Peace Pledge Union by night,' said Mr Robinson.

If I were a member of a branch of A.R.P. and on the order of a tribunal some young squirts were dumped into the branch in which I was serving I should resent it,' he continued amid loud applause.

Mr Robinson said that the vast majority of Civil Servants were 100 per cent behind the government, and were entitled to unqualified praise for their efficiency and loyalty.

'It seems a tragedy,' he commented that amongst the tens of thousands of Civil Servants there should be this small minority bringing the entire Service into disrepute by the violence of their views and their refusal to give allegiance to the Government in time of crisis.'

He quoted the observations of Civil Servants who had appeared during recent days before the Lancaster tribunal, read the reported opinion of one of the applicants that 'the dissolution of the British Empire would be a theoretical rather than an actual loss' and that a 'German domination of Europe would result in Germany ceasing to be militaristic' 'Did you even hear such tripe?' asked Robinson.

'Unfortunate Aspect'

'Now,' he went on, 'a most unfortunate aspect of this problem has presented itself. A Civil Servant who is described as joint secretary of the peace Pledge Union in Blackpool, has gone to Lancaster and asked for a private trial on the grounds that his employment would be adversely affected by publicity. (Cries of Shame.)

'His request was granted,' said Mr Robinson. 'So it comes about that a Civil Servant has been granted the privilege of a private trial. I say that is all wrong, that all applicants at courts should be treated similarly. There should be no preference given to Civil Servants or to any other class of the community.

'There are men, sincere men, who assert that their conscience will not allow them to fight or to kill, but who are prepared to volunteer in ambulance units and in such service offer themselves to their country. Such men I respect. Of such men we can be proud.

'Unfortunately, there are others who says 'No we don't want to fight, but we don't want to do anything else either because we disapprove of war and are all against it'. Yet these sane people will accept the protection which the armed forces of the Crown offer them, and eat the food that men of the merchant fleet, in face battleships submarines and the threat of bombing aeroplanes bring to these shores.

'We can have no use for such men,' said Mr Robinson amid applause.[21]

Nationally, things were moving fast: after the poorly planned and disastrous attempt to defend Norway from Nazi invasion, Chamberlain lost the confidence of the House and on 9 May 1940 he resigned in favour of Winston Churchill, Lord Halifax having felt himself unable to rise to the challenge. On the same day, presumably while all these critical discussions were taking place, the staunchly Conservative MP for Blackpool South, Roland Robinson[22] felt moved to raise the matter of Walter's case in the House of Commons:

> Mr. Roland Robinson asked the Parliamentary Secretary to the Ministry of Home Security, as representing the First Commissioner of Works, whether he is aware that the case of an employé [sic] of his Department, working at Blackpool, was heard in camera before the local tribunal for the registration of conscientious objectors at Lancaster, on the 25th April, on the grounds that his employment at the Department in which he was engaged might be adversely affected by the publicity; and whether this was done at the request of his Department?

The Parliamentary Secretary to the Ministry of Home Security (Mr. Mabane)

> My Noble Friend is aware that this case was heard in camera at the applicant's request, but does not know the reason for the request given by the applicant. The request was not made by or at the instigation of the Department.[23]

On 10 May, Germany invaded France and on the 12 May all German and Austrian males between the ages of 16 and 60 living in Britain were interned. This may well have included some of Walter's friends from Youth House.

On 11 May the Establishment Officer of the Department of Works, Mr Spencer, took action and wrote a confidential letter to Walter accusing him of taking an active part in the Peace Pledge Union and of ignoring the principles of conduct for civil servants in Establishment Leaflet No.2. and of departing from the undertaking he gave given to the Director of Lands and Accommodation at the time of his removal from St. Anne's to Blackpool.[24] As a result a Board would be convening a meeting to consider his conduct.

On 17 May Walter sent a robust reply first of all discussing his removal from St. Anne's and then protesting that he did not feel he had departed from his agreement with the director since he did not consider the PPU to be a political organisation but an ethical and philosophical one. He then emphasised that, in asking for the tribunal to be held in camera, he had been trying to minimise any embarrassment to his department and that it was Mr Robinson MP who had created the fuss by giving details to the *Gazette*. He enclosed the letter from the PPU defining his activities and added:

> With regard to the proceedings before the tribunal I should perhaps mention I am advised that, in view of the order for the case to be heard in camera, my release of copies of the evidence and findings may amount to contempt of court.

He then went firmly on the attack regarding the events that have occurred:

> Notwithstanding the overdrawn and undignified assertions of Mr. Robinson I cannot consider that my activities in Blackpool could be regarded as prejudicial to my position in the Department or contravening a fair interpretation of the principles of Establishment Leaflet No. 2. It seems from a statement made by the Editor of the Blackpool Gazette that there was a movement afoot to 'wipe out' the P.P.U. in Blackpool. Information was obtained by some means and when close investigation disclosed my connection, the greatest advantage was taken of my being a civil servant.

He finished the letter with assurance to the board that his actions in future will conform to the hitherto unrealised strictness of the rules.[25]

Walter's protests were in vain. He was dismissed, or invited to resign perhaps, from the civil service and went back to London, living in Camden Town and/or Youth House. Perhaps he was living off savings or the sale of his car. At the end of May the British army was evacuated from Dunkirk by 'the little boats of Britain'.[26] In June he took Anne for a week's stay in Norwich to meet his parents. He now proposed leaving England and going to live in Jersey but nothing came of that idea, which was fortunate since the Nazis invaded the Channel Isles on 30 June. The Battle of Britain started on 9 July and so did the so-called 'tip-and-run' raids over East Anglia—which meant mostly Norwich, Yarmouth and Lowestoft.

Notes

1. Kramer, p.37—notes a report in *The Times* (19 June 1940) that 40 per cent of Norwich City Council employees had registered as conscientious objectors, and that a *Mass Observation* study remarks that Norwich was a strong centre for pacifism.
2. See Moorehead, Caroline. *Troublesome People: The Warriors of Pacifism*, 1986, chapter 6.
3. Reported in the House of Commons 2.2 per cent of the call-up for the October 1939 registration and 2.1 per cent. for the December registration. See *Hansard* January 1940 Volume 356. Numbers decreased substantially after the fall of France in July 1940.
4. See Moorehead, chapter 7.

5. See Kramer, chapter 3.
6. Although no longer a pacifist, Fenner Brockway MP was chairman of the CBCO because he believed in freedom of conscience.
7. Walter's full statement, Appendix 2.
8. Letter from WM to WFM, 29 January 1940. In possession of the author.
9. Percy Howes, Estate Agents.
10. His father's letter is in Appendix 3. Only the accompanying letter from Eddington from 2 Christchurch Road Norwich, dated 21 February 1940 has survived.
11. 22 February 1940, *Hansard* Vol 357.
12. Conservative MP for South Kensington.
13. MP for Leyton, a Unitarian minister and brother-in-law to Fenner Brockway.
14. The full statement can be found in Appendix 3.
15. See Kramer, chapter 4.
16. A.R.P—Air Raid Precautions
17. *West Lancashire Evening Gazette*, 26 April 1940, p. 5.
18. Ibid., p. 4.
19. Letter of 25 April 1940, written from 11 Gorse Road, Blackpool.
20. The full letter can be found in Appendix 4.
21. West Lancashire Evening Gazette, Saturday 27 April, 1940, p. 3.
22. A barrister and Conservative MP for 33 years and later Governor of Bermuda. He was raised to the peerage in 1964 as Baron Martonmere.
23. *Hansard* column 1405. Debates Thursday 9 May, 1940.
24. The full letter can be found in Appendix 5.
25. The full letter can be found in Appendix 6.
26. His friend, Jack Brockway, was among those captured and held as a prisoner of war. Fortunately, he survived.

11. Summer 1940—February 1941

Now that Hitler's aims were clear for all to see, 1940 was the year that several of the prominent promoters of the peace movements changed their minds. A.A. Milne who had written *Peace With Honour* in 1934, now published *War With Honour* followed by *War Aims Unlimited*. Bertrand Russell, the great philosopher of pacifism, began to think that, faced with Nazism, war was the lesser of the two evils. The philosopher and radio broadcaster C.M. Joad who avoided conscription in World War I and chaired the National Peace Conference of 1937-8, publicly abandoned pacifism and the author and journalist Rose Macauley, another public pacifist, resigned from the Peace Pledge Union. Even that most devoted pacifist, Fenner Brockway, felt compelled to support the war although he still defended the rights of COs and continued to serve as chair of the Central Board of Conscientious Objectors until his death in 1988. Writer and broadcaster Edward Blishen, in his memoir of 1972, made the astute comment about his own pacifism, 'When I look back now, I think it was my father's war that I refused to fight.'[1]

It's not clear what Walter was doing in the early summer of 1940 except his mandatory first-aid work with the ambulance service in London. It was extremely difficult for COs to find work — unsurprisingly they were resented even, and especially, in rural areas where there was a great need for work to be done on the land.[2] The Forestry Commission had begun to employ objectors and a Christian Pacifist Forestry and Land Unit was formed.[3] Early in July, Walter left London to take up re-afforestation work at a camp called B.F. at Efail Fach near Port Talbot, in Wales. When he got there he found it didn't involve using his surveying skills or even planting trees so much as long heavy days of clearing scrub and ferns. He found the intense religiosity in the area, and perhaps even in the organisation of the camp, difficult to stomach and linked it to the economic oppression of the local people. It was not long after his arrival that his mother clearly expressed her views about faith and religion:

> I do not think God or religion has anything to do with the conditions of the peoples in Wales. They no doubt feel so deeply about things that their faith is something stronger and deeper under the conditions they live and in spite of conditions they have to cope and not knowing any thing better they make the best of it. Justice has nothing to do with God it has to do with the people concerned who are making money out of the miners like the people who own the cotton mills and make clothes to cover the savages. Organised religion is like that but without a belief in God which we get from within us there not much left whether one is poor or rich.[4]

According to a letter from one Henry Carter in *The Times* 19 May 1940 in response to a complaint about the lack of enthusiasm for manual labour from COs, in the forestry camps there were "no proper provision for housing, sanitation, or essential social amenities."[5] Walter stuck it for a while but he couldn't see the point and his father was very empathetic, writing:

> How plain every sensation of yours comes to me who experienced something very similar during 1918-1919. We have been wondering about [you] and I somehow had an idea you were for it, you were not to be employed in an advisory way so what you are doing seemed the only possible kind of employment intended.[6]

In the same letter his mother added a note urging him to come home if he wanted and added that Jack, too, was under pressure with civilian duties:

> ... he has been working overtime at his job and 2 nights each week he hasn't been home till 8 o/c and gone on LDV work all night till 6 o/c in the morning and office again at 9o/c. Do not think by that I am making comparison but it just shews how wars effect everyone and not for anyone's good.[7]

When his father sent him a bicycle Walter decided to leave and cycle back the 200 miles to London This ambitious endeavour was helped by a lift from a friendly lorry driver who came from Norfolk. Walter was back in London by 23 July.[8]

A letter from a CO co-worker, John, sent after Walter had left, described the work that they had been doing clearing scrub off a slope and told him that after all their work it had subsequently been bombed by the Germans so was more pointless than even they had conceived. John referred in a light-hearted tone to the various religious sects that tried to convert them, and sent news of other colleagues, finishing: "If anything of interest happens in the hub of the Empire, do let us, aliens in a strange land, know by letter, post-card, telegram, carrier-pigeon, or any means available. Benedictions Thine John."[9]

Walter found digs at 14 Beacon Hill, Camden Hill and was reunited with Anne. By now, in the face of the war and ostracism, they were becoming committed to each other, and Anne supported his views as did other friends from Youth House. John Gregory and Denys Val Baker stayed firm in their belief in pacifism. John Gregory managed to keep working for part of the war and then joined ENSA, Denys Val Baker became secretary of Youth House, started working as a writer which eventually became his career, and carried out rescue work in London. Others were not so minded. Robbie Sakhar, an Indian friend, had been waiting enthusiastically for war because it would bring independence for India in its wake. Bill Shepherd and his new wife Peggy went into war work as soon as they saw the UK facing defeat, presumably around 1940. He was in holy orders in the Liberal Catholic Church so "was not liable for active military service but had a distinguished career in North Kensington ARP".[10] Ralph Swingler, who married Winnie Shields in August 1941

67. Group picture taken after the Swingler-Shields wedding at Youth House August 1941.

with the reception at Youth House, worked in the technical department of Hawker Siddley, the aircraft manufacturers, so most definitely contributed to the war effort.

Walter found a job working with a health food supplier, known to his father. It was enough to keep going although his mother noted in a letter that it would hardly suit long term as she didn't think he had the right temperament for business. By contrast his father was delighted that he was associated with the cause that had defined his life. Walter evidently discussed his philosophical views with his parents throughout this period and in one letter his father restated his own position:

> ... I do not accept the material conception of history, because if you accept this you have to accept the findings of scientists and I would rather trust a simple sincere man than a collection of one-eyed theories.[11]

But he added later in the same letter:

> We who[,] in these times[,] mark time as it were must be prepared to take what such a position hand out to us but our struggle for the maintaining of those things which we regard as justice for ourselves and others must go on and it is a joy to know we are in great company.[12]

On 30 July 1940 Jennie wrote to her son about the bombing:

> My Dear Boy,
>
> Just a line in case you read the papers that we are quite safe after another bad raid early this morning about 6 o'clock. We were nearly shaken out of bed. Bombs in the Bus Station, Surrey Street, Nursing Home, Water Works Office, Dr Mills, in fact all Surrey Rd caught it. Ber St, City Rd, Cyprus Street, Harford Street and the new Estate nearby to Old Lakenham Church. It's a terrifying experience and everywhere looks terrible but am

glad to say we are alright.

A few days later she wrote again:

August 2 1940

My Dear Boy

Your letter just received and I hasten to tell you that we are through another day's raids. Early yesterday morning at 1 o/c we got a warning, all clear at 2.30 nothing happened. 3 o/c in the afternoon we got a bombing. Dad was outside the back door painting the boards he saw the plane go over and the bombs drop I was resting it shook our house and windows and I thought they had got us they dropped on Boul [Boulton] and Pauls again a terrific blaze we could hear the roaring of the fire. It even machine gunned people in the street the extent of casualties is not known yet much heavier than published at 11 o/c last night another warning till 12.30 not happened but it takes it out of one. 2 severe bombing raids in one week that makes 4 we have had in 3 weeks. I feel today like nothing on earth.

3 wks ago I fell down on Trafalgar Street and took a large piece of my knee and its very painful and is not healing very quickly I tripped in a hole in the path.

I should very much like to have seen you this week end but it is not fair to ask you during these many raids and of course I don't know if you are having a day [off] on Monday.

Dad should be in London on Wednesday but have not made up his mind yet he does not like to leave me alone.

She went on to tell him that Jack had bought his first car, a little Austin Seven Swallow for fifteen pounds, and that people were evacuating Norwich making business very uncertain. As usual she was sending a food parcel. At the end of the month she replied to a letter from him wondering if they were safe:

Yes my dear we are quite safe only very tired we spend our time getting in and out of bed and lying downstairs as comfortable as possible We sometimes get 8 or 9 alarms a day which kill business and we often get an alarm at 9.15 which lasts off and on with intervals of an ½ hour till 5 o/c in the morning. Not having a shelter we have to improvise under the table and settee.

So glad you are safe life is hectic isn't it. I had started to write this on Wednesday and then couldn't finish. We give longer news later but felt you are anxious about us. Wish you were here so we could all be together.

Sorry I haven't written before but you are always in my thoughts and when I read the papers I always remark I wonder if Walter and Ann and Fred and all my friends are safe but its rather a selfish way of thinking but [one's] own always comes first.[13]

A couple of weeks later on September 18, his father wrote to him thanking him for having sourced some honey and telling him of the disturbed days and nights they had with the bombing. He mentions an article in the *News Chronicle* about Pacifism and his disappointment in the contents of the *New Statesman* recently. He adds, with a flash of perception:

> It is curious that I should find comfort in the obvious sincerity of some parts of Churchill's speeches. I believe that is because he shows the same positiveness in his particular field of thought that I admire in my pacifism.

As he was writing the siren sounded but they were not going to respond and rush to a shelter:

> One of the misconceptions of Hitler was that we could be intimidated but I consider that all of us whether supporters of the War or not are united in so far as we would rather have death than shameful surrender.

And he added thoughtfully:

> I do hope Ann is standing up to it I am glad to get news of her I think that very often the people who are considered usually somewhat nervous are at their best when trouble really comes.

The London Blitz began on 7 September. Walter wrote home asking for a li-lo he thought he had left there and his mother, not finding it, urged him to buy another at her expense so presumably he was sleeping on a floor or camp bed. She also sent him food parcels and told him how proud they were of both their boys.

Both their boys. This was the crunch. Jack was now of age for military service. He had no clear profession or trade. He was working for the Labour Exchange and doing home Guard duty at night. He didn't want to wait to be conscripted and had already made some moves

68. *Jack at Horning, Norfolk aged about 19.*

to join the RAF—and perhaps been turned down.[14] One of his closest friends, nicknamed 'Scratch', had joined and been killed in a horrible accident in July. This was almost certainly Sergeant-Pilot J.E. Catchpole, aged 23, of 1 Ethel Road, Norwich.[15] He had only got his 'wings' the month before when he had alighted from his plane he stepped back into the propellors. Jennie had written to Walter:

> I read it in the Evening News and was watching for Jack to come home and hoping no one would blurt it out to him but that woman at the top of the road [Trafford Road] saw him and called and told him. I know how much Jack thought of him and their plans for the future. I think she might have left Jack to come home without telling him. I always have tried to take the keen edge off troubles for you both [-] it has been my duty.[16]

Jack was deeply upset but it didn't deter him and his parents knew they couldn't stop him. His father thought he was too much influenced by external events and not enough by his inner guidance. But Jack had either broken away from the Quaker thinking or not come of an age to adopt it for himself, and went to Uxbridge to enrol in October, stopping by to see Walter on his way.[17] The relentless bombing of London which eventually lasted nine months, until May 1941, was well underway.

There was bombing in Norwich, too, but the Germans often missed their targets, or bombed erratically. However, it was all very bad for business and it was hard to keep the shop going. Walter senior wrote to say how thankful they were for their car which he could use for carrying goods for shop deliveries and asked if Walter knows of a supplier of honey since he anticipated a shortage. They were well aware of the dreadful pounding that London was taking but, he remained optimistic because he felt that the outcome of the conflict would be the definite 'outlawry of War'.

During this period Walter went through considerable inner turmoil. He left the employ of the food supplier. His mother thought it might be because the proprietor was a woman and she knew he wouldn't like that. His situation was unsettled to say the least and it was probably at this time that Anne kept him for a while from her £4 a week wages, giving him half. He decided to try to get back on course and find work as a surveyor again and wrote letters to colleagues at the Chartered Surveyors' Institute to engage their support. There are not enough surviving letters to understand exactly what they could do for him but it is likely it had some effect.

Late in the year (1940) he wrote a poem about leaving the Blitz and arriving in a safe area, perhaps on a trip to Norwich, and he sent a copy to Mary.[18] Mary identified what she saw as his problem in one of her letters which she wrote as the bombs were falling[19]:

> … your letter made me very sad for I had the impression of an unsettled unhappy spirit and I wanted so much to sit down opposite you and talk hard for several hours. I know so well that in these days you may say

happiness and serenity are impossible under present conditions but there is a serenity of spirit and an inward peace that can be achieved and in which you seemed so sadly lacking. I am going to be frank even at the expense of your disliking me. I think it is a great pity that you left your job that held a little promise of a future. I know that future is an illusion nowadays but one **must** at least imagine it exists. One must go on believing in a better day allowing for all the 'ifs' and 'buts'. You have been drifting for too long now my dear. Don't let all the chaos and misery in the world affect your inward life and development. You **must** keep your soul strong—so many weak ones are going to pieces and its weak ones that have allowed all this misery to come about. You know so well that you are among the right-thinking minority — there's no need for me to tell you that, you know it so well yourself and know I'm not handing out bouquets. As such you must not drift—drifting is so weakening. I know things here are lousy—I know your own circumstances seem difficult and its ghastly to see those we love stricken and shaken but it's the common lot and as a humanitarian you must bear it with the rest. You will not do you own mind or soul a scrap of good by avoiding the trials of your fellow human-beings. While deploring fighting the awful errors of the present situation I know so surely that only by bearing them can I still feel my touch of humanity that makes me a pacifist. Wherever you can find the slightest root again STAY. Don't let the evils of the world that are opposed to your every ideal drive you out. Stay and cope with whatever comes to you. Only thus will you find peace in your heart. I know the inevitable reply to this is that the misery to other souls makes personal happiness and peace impossible but that is not so. You cannot at present stop the misery, by being strong and serene you can help those on whom misery falls.

Without religious faith, or strong spiritual core, conscientious objection was a hard position to hold and defend, especially now that Jack had joined up. But there was another factor that Mary pin-pointed but assumed was temporary: Walter's restlessness. She was not to know that this was not just a reaction to the current circumstances. It was a psychological trait, and a deep-rooted one; throughout his life he never liked 'to stay'.

Early in January 1941, Jack began his training with the Royal Air Force at Torquay. He had stayed with his Uncle Fred in London on the way down and was billeted at Downes Hotel, Babbacombe. In a letter of 16 January he described his journey:

There were about two hundred other fellows on the same train and we were met at the station and bought to Babbacombe by a truck. After supper and the filling-in of forms I was given the address of my billet and told to find my way there in the "black-out"; not a very pleasant task, you will agree, especially after a long railway journey.

I have been residing at this billet for about three days, and found it quite comfortable, although I have to go to one of the hotels for lunch. I have since been transferred to a hotel on the front as you will observe from my address.

Babbacombe is to Torquay, Walter, as St Annes is to Blackpool, it is a mass of residential hotels commandeered by the R.A.F. and occupied by thousands of potential pilots and observers, whose course lasts from two to three weeks, when they are posted to an I.T.W. [Initial Training Wing].

Significantly, as it turned out later, Jack told Walter about being vaccinated. This would have been the first time he had had any inoculation because his father, as part of his championing of natural foods, was against the practice.

I have also been inoculated and vaccinated, twice in the chest and once in the arm, as well as being blood grouped. For these hardships we received a period of 48 hr excused from duty, and I can tell you we needed it, what with feverishness and pain in the chest. Well it's all over now, and I'm quite fit again, but have the prospect of further injections in six days [sic] time.[20]

Jack described the drill and lectures and his appreciation of a letters from his mother, evidently feeling homesick. A month later he wrote:

I am still at the same old place and likely to be for perhaps another week or two. Apparently there is a hold up because of the weather being bad for flying at the E.F.T.S. [Elementary Flying Training School] the staff here seem rather at a wit's end to know what to do with us arrangements are made for two weeks only. We get about two hours drill every day, navigation lectures and sometimes a nine mile route march in the afternoons. I shall certainly be well prepared for I.T.W. [Initial Training Wing].[21]

He was still very homesick and adjusting to military life:

I bet you enjoyed going home

69. Jack aged 21 in his RAF uniform.

the other Sunday getting some decent food and I am sure Mother and Dad were pleased to see you. You are very lucky to be so comparatively near.[22]

This was a reference to the fact that Walter's efforts to gain support from the Institute of Chartered Surveyors had born fruit and he had secured a job as a senior assistant to a firm of architects headed by Harold Marsh in King's Lynn. His persistent argument was that he would be more useful to the country using his skills for land drainage in the Fens thus creating more agricultural land to feed the country, than in clearing scrub on Welsh hillsides.[23] There is no remaining evidence of who he had to persuade or how he managed it.

Despite this improvement in his working life, Walter evidently wrote complaining about the long winter days out on the Fens and Jack replied:

> I am glad to hear you are OK if rather stiff from the strenuous nature of your work. It isn't too good having to turn out in all weathers, but as long as you see after yourself it should make you pretty tough and keep you fit. It is very much the same down here, especially when one has a twenty-four-hour guard duty and there's snow about.
>
> The staff seem rather at a wit's end to know what to do with us, as bad weather holding up flying, also holds up the clearance of people who have finished the I.T.W. course yesterday some of my flight went to the flight officer to try to get a day or two's leave for us; but without success. No leave except on compassionate grounds. This is because of the uncertainty of posting. There is an intake of about three hundred here every week and we are all hoping that the problem of accommodation will force them to do something, if we are kept here much longer.

Jack was hoping he might get sent to Cambridge and complained of the lack of female company. He wondered if Walter was going to move flats but noted that he should perhaps get permission from 'the old man', a sign of how much they were both still under his authority. Jack himself had very little money and often not even enough to phone home as much as he would like. He adds: "I never thought I should miss you all as much as I do. Well my boy, I can't give you any advice but that you are lucky to be able to work and to have something to work for."[24]

During the winter of 1940–41 women aged 21–30 were called to active service and Anne registered as a conscientious objector.

Notes

1. Blishen, Edward, *A Cack-handed War*, 1972, p. 228.
2. Ibid.
3. See Goodall.
4. Letter from Jennie to Walter F., 21 August 1940.
5. Quoted in: Breech, Allyson. *Conscientious Objectors During Britain's Last Popular War*.

University Paper 1998-9, Texas and A & M University, Department of History.
6. Letter of midsummer 1940, undated.
7. Ibid.
8. Dated by a letter from his mother.
9. Letter 4, August 1940.
10. Information from his son Martin W. Shepherd by email.
11. Letter undated but referring to Walter's work and a week that Walter F and Anne had spent in Norwich.
12. Ibid.
13. Letter of August 28 1940.
14. He enlisted with his friend Ken Holmes, later to become business editor of the *Eastern Daily Press*.
15. *Norwich Evening News*, 22 July, 1940, p. 2, Death Notice. He was the husband of Pat, née Goulder.
16. Letter of July 23 1940. Jennie to Walter F.
17. His uncle, Fred Swann, wrote to him, 'I am pleased to see we've got two soldiers in the family and of two generations.'
18. See Appendix 2 for the full poem.
19. Undated but identifiable as from late in the year.
20. Letter of 16 January 1941. Walter too, much later, had extreme reactions to vaccines.
21. Letter from Jack, 12 February 1941.
22. Ibid.
23. Drainage of the Fens, starting in the 17th century, has now been reassessed as a major ecological tragedy.
24. Letter from Jack to A&W, 25 February 1941.

12. February 1941—May 1942

Walter moved first to some digs near the King's Lynn railway station and when Anne soon followed, they found a flat at 20 Harecroft Gardens. He received a long letter from his father asking whether he intended to get married and suggesting he would be wise to get into a better financial position.[1] A few days later his mother wrote in a softer tone showing that she understood the need for companionship, and incidentally giving a glimpse into her own married life:

> I hope neither of you will ever feel so lonely as I do but I have to make the best of it the same as I have done all my life. I don't think Dad sees things quite the same as I do. I tell him he must not query anything just let you and Ann make your own arrangements. You have reached the age of discretion and you were fortunate in having people like 'Mary' and Ann when you first left home.[2]

Not only had both her boys left home but her husband, Walter, was often out on long stints of fire watching. She added:

> Business is getting very difficult in fact I don't tell Dad I am getting rather concerned because we cannot replace stocks which are running very low so many of our principle lines have entirely finished. Nuts are running out no replacement the same with olive oil, Dried Fruits — Bananas. All nut fats. We have had a few dates the last week but the profits are government control[sic] so they really are not much to us. Biscuits we cannot get for love nor money. … Tea we get about 1/3 our usual supply so things are not rosy for us after 26 years of hard work. Still we must keep going if we can The Health Food Stores must keep going somehow. Trade is good if only we can get supplies….
>
> Now my dear go ahead and keep smiling you have had very few disappointments so far and I hope you will not have many. Life is not a bed of roses, but we must do all we can to make it so. Share with us any troubles and we will do our best for you.
>
> All my love
>
> Mother[3]

News travelled fast round the family and Walter had been letting off steam again about his working conditions and how fed up he was, but Jack, now well into his military training, wasn't about to let him get away with it. He wrote from the Sergeant's Mess at RAF Juby on the Isle of Man at the beginning of March:

Dear Walter and Anne

I have just heard from home that Walter is feeling 'browned off' with overwork, so I thought I had better take the initiative in renewing our postal acquaintances. Looking at it in a brotherly spirit I have been wondering what to say to make you feel better, Walter. It is, however, impossible to say anything or give a simple solution in a few words. Alternatively I could say "Well, who isn't browned off" and then proceed to give such a list of my own misfortunes as to make your own petty worries appear as flea bites. Therefore I will continue this letter without comment expounding unto you the "gen" and hoping you may benefit. By the way Anne I do not know what your feelings are, on this subject. I am sure, however, that Walter would be far more "browned off" is you weren't there to spoil the cakes. It is a great thing to have a good companion in life. Two shoulders are better than one.

There are very few people who cannot give one thousand reasons for being "browned off". We have all one thousand and one reasons for being thankful some of us more than others. It is up to everyone, therefore, to carry on as best as they can until we can put matters right.

Jack had his own problems and ones that foreshadowed the future. The pilots were under constant pressure from their superiors and the planes they were flying were not up to scratch. With a shortage of planes, the best were kept for the fighter pilots, the ones used in training were often damaged.

Now that's off my chest I have to admit I am rather "browned off" myself. Since being back I have been transferred to Navigation Flight, which although more interesting has its drawbacks. Firstly, the pupils who navigate the plane cannot always be relied upon. We are "chewed up" if we turn back too often through bad weather. Each pilot has his own wireless op: air gunner but the wirelesses are seldom serviceable. The aircraft are ex operational ones and some of them not too reliable. Lastly, whatever happens the pilot takes the blame.

He had had to make a crash landing but fortunately no one was hurt:

Last week the engines packed in over North Wales but I got down in a field O.K. near Penhios. Bent the aircraft a bit but no one inside it. A couple of weeks ago two of our machines came down on mountains here, while night flying. One of them was my pal Henderson from I.T.W. EFTS days. Luckily he got away with broken nose and arm; but two of the crew were killed

Well I am sorry the news is not a little more cheerful but don't worry I am O.K. But I shall not be if I don't get some leave soon.

...

I am looking forward to seeing you both in the near future, in the meantime keep cheerful

Love and best wishes Jack[4]

Whether from parental pressure or not, Anne and Walter decided get married. They would have chosen a registry office wedding but, in another letter, Walter senior—the Governor—emphasized the importance of marriage as a sacred institution and they bowed to his wishes. Jack had had a stroke of luck, or managed 'to wangle' a posting to Cambridge ['A' Flight No 2 Squadron] and was fortunate enough to be billeted in Trinity Hall which he enjoyed. He wrote to Walter towards the end of March 1941:

> I hear from mother that it is your intention to get married in the near future. All I can say to that is to wish both you and Anne the very best of luck and every happiness. You will most probably be seeing mother and the Guv'nor to-day and they will probably inform you of my desire to be present at the ceremony and if possible to be best man. I should like to know how this appeals to you and if so to fix a date so I can try and wangle some leave.[5]

Jack had been taking his exams and come out with top marks. Now he was free to concentrate on navigation.[6]

Walter wrote to Jack,[7] formally asking him to be his best man. Jack replied:

> You will be pleased to know that I have succeeded in obtaining a pass from 10.30 hours on Saturday until 23.59 hours Sunday.
>
> ...
>
> What's more to the point however is this: - the sergeant here says he will arrange to get me off after lunch Friday, if I can fix it with the navigation officer. All being well I should be able to manage this.[8]

Anne and Walter married on 5 April 1941 at St Margaret's Kings Lynn, a large church for a small wedding. Jack and Jennie were the only people attending. It was a Saturday and Walter senior had to mind the shop. Anne wore a black suit.

At the end of April 1941 Jennie wrote to say that Jack was being reposted to flying school and was at home on a short leave. While she was writing, bombs began falling on Norwich:

> We have just had a terrific shock I cannot write plainly I am shaking so [,] bombs have dropped pretty close. I don't quite know where but they have given us a shake up. There is a huge fire and Jack is out we can see the flames at the back terrific. They got Horning Ferry Sunday night about 20 killed and more than that number seriously wounded.

Tomkins [neighbour presumably] has just knocked at the door its 10 past 11 and Jack has gone to see if he can help. Carrow has been hit. Bracondale School the Dormitory is cut quite off. I shall know more later.

Jack is home the fire is very bad they hit Carrow Works and Carrow Hill and lots of houses in that vicinity. The school is not so bad as at first feared luckily there are very few boarders. The school reopens next week. It is an awful business I heard the bombs whizzing through the air and then they dropped incendiary ones as well.'[9]

Jack was posted to various air bases, trained to fly and then started training other recruits from the Isle of Man. Walter stayed working for Marsh in King's Lynn and the bombing of Norwich continued intermittently There are no further surviving letters until nearly a year later when Jennie relayed to Anne and Walter news of Jack having again crash landed in Wales:

70. Interior of St Margaret's Church, King's Lynn. Postcard.

> We had a letter from Jack last Tuesday in which he told us of an experience he had luckily he and his pupil came out of it without a scratch. He had to make a forced landing in Nth Wales owing to engine trouble the under carriage of the plane was damaged in landing but he landed quite safely near a farm. The farmer Jack says he will never forget his kindness nor the Welsh people. What with cups of tea etc the luncheon they sent out on the field to the pupil with whom Jack had leave in charge of the plane and the farmer driving Jack to the village and back was really wonderful, and Jack is now safely back in Jurby. I think he had a miraculous escape.
>
> He is looking forward to his leave very much he say he don't know of anything else he have looked to in his life so I hope we shall all meet and give him a good holiday.[10]

The rest of the lengthy letter is about shortages in the shops and of supplies for the Health Food Store and the difficulties of trying to keep the shop running with insufficient staff and how hard it was for them both.

On 19 March 1942 Walter senior wrote to Walter and Anne, probably in response to some qualms or difficulties they were experiencing, about Walter's position as a CO with regard to the Home Guard and set out the pacifist position again:

> I feel that we pacifists should be prepared for criticism and should expect opposition. I do not know if some of the personal contacts you have made are with those who are sympathetic but if you do not meet opposition at some time or another you will be exceptional. I do think that it is not wise to go out of your way to raise opposition. I believe in sticking to one's principle but give the uttermost latitude to opinions, one's actions show one's principles. It may be that Marsh himself may make it convenient and raise the question which would be the best way for both of you. I like to think that his opinion of your services would outweigh such things as opposition to your opinions as to War. We are supposed to be fighting for the individual right of opinion and this to my mind is the main reason why we shall eventually win. This right of opinion is the very spirit of the Allied Nations and this is the strongest moral link in the chain which binds both those who agree with war and those who do not.[11]

He went on to underline that it was because of the essential right to opinion that they as a family, also honoured Jack—he had made his own choice. Walter added "and I love my country because it stands out miles ahead of any other in this matter."

He finished by advising his son Walter to cultivate an equable state of mind and to find some interests that will help reduce his worry. They were expecting to hear from Jack about forthcoming leave. But then a new danger hit Norwich—the Baedeker raids. Jennie wrote to Jack on 29 April 1942:

> … I don't know how quickly news spread to the I.O.M. but on Monday night we had a most trying experience. In fact for over 2 hours a "Hell of a Time" at 11.35 the warning went we had got to bed a little earlier that night so we laid in a bit thinking perhaps they were not coming our way. All at once the bombing starting [sic] we rushed up and dressed we hadn't time to get to the shelter. Dive bombing. Machine gunning. H.E. Explosions bombs and flares were continuance [sic] over a very wide area. Residential areas and poorer streets have got it badly there's is no Victoria Station nor City Station left. Wincarnis 2 breweries. Poor Law Infirmary. Blind Institution 2 other schools. Your heart would ache to see poor old Norwich. The Casualty is not yet known. Some of the fires are still burning it is estimated 20,000 homeless everything is being done as quickly as possible for them. Poor Mr and Mrs Moore [family friends]

their home is just a heap they have lost nearly everything. Winifred [their daughter] I hear is in a terrible state. At present they are all at Connaught Road [No 51, home of Hamilton and Tilly]. I offered them my room and we are going to Connaught Road after Dad comes home to see if we can do anything for them.

… Nearer home bombs dropped between the Parish Room and the church. Our house on Trafford Rd is the only one which haven't a window out somewhere even Mrs Leary's front bedroom window was blown out and ours are intact isn't it wonderful. Today is the first day I have been to the City since Saturday. The scene of destruction is widespread but that's really nothing in comparison to lives lost. The Smiths have all their windows out.

After the All-Clear Dad went to the shop and everything there was all right. We really thought there would have been some damage. Buntings. Curl bros, Saxon, most of the shops on the Walk The Gas Company hundreds of places too numerous to mention. Piles of glass all over the place.

They tried to get through last night and came 2 hours later we went into the shelter gun firing was very heavy they raided "York" isn't it wonderful Jack dear we escaped. Walter and Anne came over from King's Lynn especially last night and wanted to take me back with them for a time. Whatever happens my dear I couldn't leave Dad it wouldn't be fair he would be so lonely it was extremely good of them to come all that way they only stayed about an hour.

Your photographs have not come yet. Will call on Friday to see if they are ready. It was lovely to see you again although it was a short visit. What a week we had, your visit A visit to Walter and Anne a Heavy raid and then another visit from Walter and Anne.[12]

On 4 May she wrote:

My Dearest Jack

I didn't think when you were with us a few days ago we would been through that which we have. But thank God my dear that we are alive. I only hope we shall not get anymore Raids. Poor Old City of Norwich. I feel it very deeply but she will come through alright my dear and we hope we shall live to see it.

I will not enumerate on individual places because I don't know the extension of it all but it's a vast area one or two only, there is no Orford Place, CEYM gone as houses beyond the Bowling Green Trafford Road and from Rowington Rd to the Trafford Arms so I will leave you to guess only a small portion of the damage. We are going to Mrs Ardern's [family friends,

71. The Wincarnis Factory, Westwick Street, up in flames.

Mary and Venice] every night and coming home in the morning since last Thursday and are doing so till after next Sunday. I haven't been able to call for your photos yet but will try today. I got your letter in which you say you arrived back safely. It was lovely to see you again. Dad said it was the plane which circled round the house and we came inside to look at you.[13]

On 5 May she wrote again because the bombing continued and it was unsafe to stay in the city centre at night. Offers of help came in from friends in Attleborough and Dereham but Jennie chose to stay with their friends the Arderns in Ringland which was closer.

I went to Ringland on Thursday as Dad was Firewatching all night. I couldn't possibly face it alone and we are going there each night and coming home in the morning and they are both extremely kind and we can do that as long as we like. We shall probably continue until after Sunday night and then make up our minds I felt I couldn't stay another night. 47 [Trafford Road] have got windows out and roof lifted but they have been repaired the windows are not put in yet they will I'm afraid be rubbering for a time but that will not matter. There are no houses the other side beyond the Bowling Green and yet from Rowington Road to the Trafford the Smiths have got ceilings down, now windows and they have gone away. But the destruction in the City is worse and isn't it fortunate my dear we are still there. We certainly thought on Wednesday night there would be no City left.[14]

Other members of the family, Hamilton and Tilly had to leave their house in Connaught Rd because it was unsafe and went to stay with a Coleman family in Water Lane, Costessey. Annie also went to Costessey but unfortunately broke her leg in the scramble to leave and ended up briefly in hospital but they wouldn't keep her in. On 7 May 1942 Jack wrote to Anne and Walter from Juby in the Isle of Man saying how glad he was that their parents were safe and that Walter had been able to get over to Norwich to look out for them. He was grateful for his recent leave home although it was all too short, "but it was worth it to see the smile on Mother's face." He went on to tell them:

> I also landed at Sutton Bridge on the way back but I am afraid I could not come to see you, although I should like to have wangled it. I am also afraid that the idea is now off as we have started a seven-day week.
>
> I am afraid things are getting less easy at Jurby. The whole cause of the trouble seems to be that another A.O.S. [Air Observer's School] had completed more flying hours for last month than we. As we are usually top in this respect the Group Captain is rather annoyed and has started a general slave drive. i.e., No breakfast after 7.30 am.
>
> P.T. at 6.30. General parade at 7.50. Another by 8.30, and a seven-day week.
>
> With the fine weather and long evenings it has been 7.30 pm or 8pm all last week before getting in for tea. This is apart from other duties and being my own housewife. I expect things are pretty tough for you too.
>
> At the present moment I am making the best of 48 hours off after inoculation. I felt pretty lousy yesterday but I am better today, so have been trying to catch up on mail question.[15]

The inoculations were necessary because he was preparing to be posted abroad to South Africa to train pilots there. He was very close to being in a safer environment but just three days later on the 10 May 1942 his luck ran out. For the third time the plane in which he was training new observers suffered from mechanical damage but this time he was not in Wales but in the deep glens of Scotland. The aeroplane was a Blenheim Mk IV from the Air Observers School at RAF Juby on the Isle of Man. Jack was the pilot with three other airmen on board: a wireless operator, Sergeant James William Chadwick, and two trainee observers, Leading Aircraftman Percival Clarke Christian and Leading Aircraftman Richard Owen Lloyd. Not all of the causes of the crash are known but a contributory factor, and the one cited on the official report, was that part of an engine cowling broke away resulting in one Engine Failure. As Jack had already written after the earlier incidents, training planes were far from being in the best condition, the pupils who navigated could not always be relied upon, and there was pressure to carry on even in bad weather. There is also the possibility that he was still suffering from a reaction to inoculation. The plane crashed into the hills at Posso Farm, near

Peebles, Scotland at 11.05 hours with the loss of all personnel aboard. The bodies were taken to RAF Turnhouse in Edinburgh. The official report also noted that the pilot had carried out the same exercise on various occasions and was therefore capable of doing so again and, so, laid responsibility on his 'Insufficiently quick reaction'.[16] This allocation of blame was exactly what Jack had noted in his previous crash landings—that the pilot was always at fault. The RAF was hardly likely to advertise that they were sending trainees up in unsafe aircraft or, for that matter, that the competition between squadrons in the Air Observer's Schools was pushing personnel to their limits.

Jack was buried at St. John the Baptist and All Saints, Old Lakenham, Norwich—Jennie's parish church from childhood. She and Walter were offered an RAF funeral but they seem to have declined although there may have been an RAF escort. There is a dedicated section of War Graves in the cemetery but Jack is not buried there. His grave is in the civilian section close to members of his mother's family.

༄༅

Notes

1. Letter from WM to WFM, 16 February 1941.
2. Letter from Jennie to WFM, 24 February 1941.
3. Letter from Jennie to WFM ,1 February 1941.
4. Letter from Jack to Anne and Walter, 2 March 1941.
5. Letter from Jack to Anne and Walter, 23 March 1941.
6. Letter from Jack to WFM, 23 March 1941.
7. He qualified as a pilot September 1941.
8. Letter from Jack to WFM.
9. Letter from Jennie to Anne and Walter, 29 April 1941.
10. Letter from Jennie to Anne and Walter 8 March 1942.
11. Letter from WM to WFM. 'You do not mention if you take a prominent part in public organisations. If you do I should consider that these would be what would mostly affect Marsh especially if you declare your opinions publicly. You experiences at Blackpool prove this.'
12. Letter from Jennie to Jack, 29 April 1942.
13. Letter from Jennie to Jack, 4 May 1942.
14. Letter from Jennie to Jack, 5 May 1942.
15. Letter from Jack to Anne and Walter, 7 May 1942.
16. Information from the Aircraft Accident Record Card 7636 received in a letter to the author from the MOD, 20 April 2022.

Afterword

All That We Are Not Stares Back at What We Are.

W.H. Auden

Jennie never recovered her health and died on 7 May 1951. Her death certificate cited heart failure, arterio-sclerosis and tuberculous polyserositis but she died close to the date of Jack's accident and those around her thought her decline was caused by shock and grief. Walter senior carried on running the Health Food Store alone until his retirement at the age of 82 in 1967 and died at the age of 92. Towards the end he told me that he felt Jack had been too young to make a considered choice between joining up or becoming a conscientious objector; it was still very much on his mind.

Anne and Walter decided to have a baby, not as replacement for Jack, but to bring new life into the family. Jonathan was born in January 1944. After a long period working on surveying in the fens for land drainage Walter designed some workers' cottages for the Sandringham Estate and then extensive public housing. After the war, through his old friend from Youth House days, Jimmy Haynes Dixon, he found work in London at the Central Office of Information and was involved in the exhibition work for the Festival of Britain which brought him into contact with a wide range of designers and architects. Life began again. He then went to work for London County Council, studying in the evenings for a degree in Town Planning from London University. I was born in 1949. We emigrated to Canada in 1956 and Harry Arnold's forecast that Walter would do well in municipal service was fulfilled. However, his restlessness continued and was never resolved.

72. *Walter Manthorpe serving in his health food shop in the 1960s.*

I am not offering any particular conclusion. I have just put down what happened as far as I can discern from the documents available. The argument against pacifism in the 1930s is that the emergence of multiple anti-war initiatives only served to unnerve the public and delay the inevitable. When it came to the crunch the public generally came down on the side of the 'just war'. Pacifists may not have been willing to kill, but many others were willing to die to stop fascism and that, implicitly, included defending the freedom to dissent.

Pacifists take a longer view. They do not consider war a natural or necessary human activity. They know that it is entrenched politically and economically but believe that it is only by the efforts of individuals and small groups that it will be challenged and eventually found to be unsatisfactory. They affirm the validity of the individual's inner life, spiritual or intellectual, to question the authority of the communal or collective.

The COs of the 1914-18 war, a very small minority of the population, held open the doors for future generations and were willing to forego their own freedom, health and livelihood to do so. After the Treaty of Versailles, the Western world was a much more complex place. Pacifism was no longer just the preserve of people with extreme religious or political views; objection to war and conscription became a valid choice for a much wider constituency of people concerned with politics. Since then, we have seen the CND marches of the 1950s and 60s, the anti-Vietnam protests of the 1970s, the Greenham Common occupation of the 1980s and 90s and the mass public demonstrations against the Iraq War in 2003. All of these gave a loud public voice to concerns about the cruelty, injustice and wastefulness of war, not to mention the long-term effects, moral, economic and physical, on individuals and on civil life, and as much for the victors as the defeated. Young men, through their idealism, are easily weaponised by older politicians. As we become more and more dependent on each other for global survival, pacifism may again find its time and its advocates, but no doubt in some new way.

As I said in the introduction, this is a Norwich story so I will leave the last words to nurse Edith Cavell who, all those years ago, shopped for her groceries at Eddington's on The Walk. In her hospital in Belgium she attended to wounded men on both sides of the conflict. Her actions were shaped by her Christian morality as was her view that: 'Patriotism is not enough.'

Victoria Manthorpe, Norwich, July 2023

Appendix 1

List of Youth House members made in 1996 by Jessica Etherington former secretary of Youth House. (*Theo. Society / TS. = Theosophical Society*)

Last name	First name	Notes
English	M V, Mrs	Theo. Society. Nickname 'Lucifer'. Founder Member, Debenture Holder
Mitchell	Elsie, Mrs	TS. Nickname 'Mike'. Founder Member, Debenture Holder
Reilly	Gerard	TS. Nickname 'Nunc'. Founder Member, Debenture Holder
Dermot	Commander	TS. Founder Member, Debenture Holder
Dermot	Catherine	TS. Founder Member, Debenture Holder
Lane	Margaret	TS. Nick name 'Pan'. Founder Member, Debenture Holder
Gregson, Mrs		TS. Nickname 'Greg'. Founder Member, Debenture Holder
English	Barbara	TS. Nickname 'Babs'
Wilkinson		TS. Nickname 'Shakespeare'
Wilkinson		TS. Nickname 'Tennyson'
Reilly	Michael	Nickname 'Reilly'
Reilly	Myra	née Jones
Churchward	Robert	'Bob'. Quaker
Dowell	Lily	
Baum	Sadie	Animal Sanctuary and NCPCA
Baum	Claire	
	Len	
Evans	Frank	
Evans	F	

Koutane	Netta	Russian
Gethman	Katie	Russian
Gethman	Alyosha	Russian
Parry	Ruth	now Pearce
Tagore	Subir	A nephew of Rabindranath Tagore
Schmidt	Dorrie	
Pereira	R	Economist
Myrtle	Holly	
Branson	David	Pianist
Grundy	Ursula	
Jackman	Frank	Architect
Stemman	Gladys	
Banfield	Bernard	
Stemman	Elsie	
Douet	Georges	French
Knights	Winnie	
Gossweiler	Paulo	Swiss
Diserens	Henri	Swiss
Diserens	Ruth	Swiss
Pinchin	Chris	Theosophical Society
Pinchin	his sister	
Tompkins	Harold	
Tompkins	his wife	
Lake	Nora	
Lake	her sister	
Samson	Lucien	French
Samson	Mariette	French
Genevieve		
Midge		
Harald		

Yi-Min		1932 Three charming young men from Communist China
		2 young men from Lebanon
Celia		Women's Suffrage - now Mrs Pankhurst. Staff member
Atkinson	Molly	
Shepherd	Peggy née Smith	Theosophical Society
Zimmerman	Ernst	Swiss
Pezaro	Leo	Dutch
Alma	Mies	Dutch
Behrens	Bernarde	
Spijker	Nico	
Spijker	Zette	
Temerlies	Joan	Staff member
Sheringham	Dorothy	
Kitchen	Beatrice	Staff member
Hutchinson	Marjorie	
Hill	Bernard	
	Win	Staff member
Swinglers	Ralph	TS. Married Win
	Anne	Staff member
	Louie	Staff member
	Edna	Staff member
Etherington	Jessica	Staff member. Nee Grimm
Indira	Jeremy	Indian
Lakhani		Indian
Sakhar	Robbie	Indian
	Vera	

Gale	Joan	TS.
Hempsted	David	TS.
Bose	Aurobindo	TS.
Pereira		TS.
Davies	Gwyn	
Clotsworthy	Maritza	AS Neil School
Zorian	Olive	Zorian String Quartet
Dienes	Zed	Dartington Hall (maths professor in Australia)
Robson	David	Dartington Hall + 9 others
Vaughan	Henry	Advertising
Vaughan	Patricia	
Hutchinson	Arthur	
Etherington	Dorothy	
MD		Actor
Val Baker	Denys	Cornwall Author
	Pat	
	Jane	Staff member
Rogers	Ken	
Miller	Joan	A Staff member
		Eric Chandler was Peggy's boyfriend
Manthorpe	Walter	
	Ann	Parker
Hammond	Ernst	
	Marguerite	
Osmond	Leslie	
	Joan	Pat
Rogers	Ken	
	Diana	
Legelli	Joan	Judy
Miller	Joan	

	Tom	
	Rosalind	
	Richard	
Manelli	Aleck	
	Winnifred	
	Ben	
	Rene	
Guest-Smith	Charles	
	Cyril	
Buckingham	Robert	
Hesse	Heinrich	German
Maine	Kurt	German
Mainz	Otto	German
Behre	Wolfgang	
Jablonsav	Wolfgang	
Mohrmanv	Lisezogte	
Pressberger	Hilda	
Pressberger	Kurt	
	Hualt	
	Kathleen	
Austin	Jack	
	Tilly	
	Stan	
Forster	Suzi	Quaker
Forster	sister	
Hahn	Ursula	
Ehrhann	Franzi	Possible Nazi spy [sic]
Popik	Max	TS.
Hirschorn	Henri	
Spivak	Henry	Polish

Dxxxxx	Michael	[surname unreadable]
Amory	Mary	
Jeffres	Ted	
	Daphne	
	Eric	
	Doris	
Chavasse	Harry	[or possibly Chavassg]
	Herthe	
Green	Sam	
	Lilt	Quaker
Brod	Mark	
Elsas	Madeleine	
	Elfreda	
Lepper	Buffy	
	Ann	
	Stella	
Carter	Harold	New Zealand
Caus	Don(?)	
Coward	John	
James	Gwyn	
Gwladys	David	

Appendix 2

Walter's Full Statement Of Objection.

27 February 1940

My objection to taking part in this or any war is based upon moral principles. These spring from a two-fold conviction: -

a. My belief that humanity is intrinsically a unity and that one man is no different from another—different in that he is not also a member of humanity.

b. My belief that the intrinsic unity is inviolable.

I am convinced that the moral principles arising from these beliefs are absolute and that one should do what is right, not what appears to be expedient. I can on no account, therefore, assume the responsibility for taking the life of a fellow-being.

I am convinced that likewise the state is not incapable of committing theft, murder or perjury, in the sense that these are moral offences. I cannot, therefore, be a party to such action. Individually, I recognise that I am a member of a political organisation—the state—to which I owe some allegiance, but at the same time I am also a member of a larger and all-embracing association, namely the human race, to which I must give the greater allegiance.

All my life both within the state and the home it has been made clear to me that to act amorally towards one's fellows is wrong, and indeed foolish. I embrace that principle but in doing so I cannot do other than carry it out in all circumstances.

I realise there are ideas abroad to-day which are a menace to the future of humanity: I know that sacrifices are essential in order to remove that menace but I cannot believe they are sacrifices to war, because war is itself an expression of that violence, hatred and corruption that it seeks to eradicate. I cannot believe that a shell fired from one direction is any more righteous than a shell fired from the opposite direction—although the combatants may be actuated by different motives, both actions are wrong and both a crime against humanity. Nor can I believe that bad means will ever achieve good ends. I am therefore convinced that the ideals of democracy cannot be safeguarded by war.

This situation has its origin in my early training and home life. Although I was not aware until I reached the age of nearly 17 years that my father was a pacifist as such and that he had been a conscientious objector to the last war, I realised than that my upbringing had been profoundly influenced by his philosophy.

My beliefs have expressed themselves in an attempt to work for peace and for the propagation of all those moral ideas which I sincerely feel are necessary for true peace. To this end I have lived for two years in a community of young people of all nations, many of whom are also pacifists, and who have created an example of mutual confidence and responsibility. As a member of this community I was naturally engaged in projects, such as the entertainment of poor children and the running of a hostel for refugees and an international hostel, expressing the essential principle of service to mankind.

As a member of the peace Pledge Union I was engaged in campaigns of literature distribution, the organisation of public meetings and, when conscription was introduced, in a house to house survey of a constituency in North West London for the purpose of ascertaining the slum-dweller's reaction to that measure. More recently I have become joint secretary of the Blackpool group of the P.P.U. and been active in leading a series of discussions on the essential philosophy of pacifism. The creation of communities for pacifist who are now workless has provided me with an opportunity of giving them some regular financial assistance.

In the theatre I have been concerned with the production of plays of social significance, bearing on the ideas which I hold.

In view of this statement, therefore, I ask that the Tribunal grants me complete exemption from the provisions of the National Service Act, since I must completely reject the principle of the law of compulsion for war purposes.

27th February 1940

Appendix 3

Letter of Support from Walter senior.

Notwithstanding the statement made by W.F. Manthorpe who being of age and capable of expressing a mature explanation of his conscience I can do no other than state that I believe it to be a true reflex of his actions and conduct and has been ever since he has been able to express belief in deeds. He was born during the stress of the last War I his father determined then that War was futile, that came what would there would be no compromise with it and in that atmosphere the consciousness of our family has developed against War. My association with the conscientious objectors of the last War continued unbroken with them including George Lansbury and the late Canon Dick Sheppard, and my active membership of both the No More War Movement and the Peace Pledge union testify to the environment of the whole life of W F Manthorpe. The State has recognised the freedom of conscience as an essential part of its Constitution and we who hold to this principle believe it to be the corner stone of the future edifice of civilisation. Believing in the Brotherhood of man and the Fatherhood of God and the inevitability of Death to those that take the sword either actually or by proxy I would understandingly support the testimony submitted by W F Manthorpe.

W Manthorpe Senior

Appendix 4

PPU statement.

26th April 1940

To Whom It May Concern.

I would say that Walter Manthorpe is not the Secretary of the Blackpool Group of the Peace Pledge Union. He did accept joint secretaryship for a period of approximately six weeks (terminating 14 April 1940) this merely entailing a small amount of correspondence work within the limits of the Group. Never at any time during his connection with this Group has he been concerned with the dissemination of pacifist propaganda, so far as I am aware.

Although invited and even pressed to speak at Pacifist Public Meetings in Blackpool and in another town, he did, on both occasions, decline to take part.

Mr Manthorpe did, on alternate Monday evenings (for a short time) open a discussion circle held in the Society of Friends' Meeting House in Raikes-parade, Blackpool, the discussion revolving round the philosophies of Socrates and Plato.

To my knowledge (and I have been most intimately concerned with the group's activities during the past few months) Mr. Manthorpe has interviewed only one person (a copyist) whilst he has been in the group, to whom, I believe, Mr. Manthorpe did not give his name.

In all conversations at which I have been present, and in his conversation generally with the group, Mr. Manthorpe has preserved the utmost discretion, to such effect that only a small circle of acquaintances were even aware of his vocation; nor has he ever impressed me as being a person who would ostentatiously try to persuade his views upon others.

Reginald S. Baxter

Ex-Secretary

Appendix 5

Memorandum regarding Walter's PPU activities.

Mr Manthorpe.

You will remember that the Director of Lands and Accommodation, after complaints had been received of your political activities at Lytham St. Annes, obtained an undertaking from you in December last to the effect that you would cease from participation in such activities. Your attention was also called to the board's regulations on the subject set out in Establishment Leaflet No. 2. As considerable embarrassment had been caused to the Department by reason of your conduct, you were then moved from Lytham St. Annes to Blackpool, and it is understood that you gave Mr Hoctor an undertaking similar to that mentioned above.

It has been reported to the Board that in spite of these undertakings you have since that time taken a considerable part in the activities of the Peace Pledge Union, and the following is an extract from the evidence which you yourself submitted to the local Tribunal for the Registration of Conscientious Objectors on the 25th April: -

"I have become joint secretary of the Blackpool Group of the Peace Pledge Union and have been active in leading a series of discussions on the essential philosophy of Pacifism."

In addition it has been reported to the board that you took the chair at a meeting of the Peace Pledge union on the 13th March, and that at another meeting on the 10th April you were the speaker.

These are apparently but instances of your conduct at Blackpool which has caused considerable embarrassment to the Department. Before deciding on what action should be taken in the matter, the board will be prepared to consider any representations you may care to make in explanation: -

1. Of your ignoring the principles of conduct laid down for your guidance in Establishment Leaflet No.2.

2. Of your departure from the undertaking given to the Director of Lands and Accommodation.

One copy of this memorandum should be signed and returned with your reply, which should be sent without delay.

Appendix 6

Walter's letter to Mr Spencer.

Mr. Spencer (Establishment)

I have to reply to your minute of the 11th instant.

In considering this matter, which I assume has arisen as the result of representations by Mr. R. Robinson, M.P. for Blackpool, I shall be glad if the board will take into account the following circumstances, and allow me first to reply to (2) of your minute.

The circumstances surrounding my removal from St Annes are still to me largely unknown, apart from the fact that some person had become aware of my opinions and because of this it was considered advisable that I should be transferred to Blackpool. I was engaged in no activities in St. Annes and although I have friends there with whom discussion naturally took place I could not remember having ostentatiously and indiscreetly publicised my views. However, it appears to me that the position was brought to the notice of the Town Clerk of St Annes and at an interview with the Director of Lands and Accommodation it was understood that I would in future take every precaution to prevent my private life of ideas conflicting with my official duties. There was no question of any activities and my impression of the matter was that an inopportune remark had, in a small town, been seized upon at a time when the actions of the Department were not being received in a favourable manner. I would, however, emphasise the fact that my relationships both with the members of the profession whom I met officially and with a circle of personal friends were of an extremely amicable nature. In particular I should perhaps mention that I stayed for a considerable period at the home of the secretary of the St. Anne's hotel owners' Association and that my strong friendship with the family continues unbroken.

At Blackpool I resolved not to express any opinion in company connected with my official activities and my private life was divorced from my work in the Department. In the circumstances I do not feel that I departed from the understanding reached with Director.

In dealing with the peace Pledge Union It is my impression that this is not a political organisation within the principles laid down in Establishment Leaflet No. 2. The society is basically an ethical and philosophical one with a religious element and it can only be termed political in so far as any association which is concerned with human behaviour can be so named. In Blackpool this religious element consisting of members of the Society of Friends is uppermost in quite a small group and for this reason my connection is not a very close one.

The press had not mentioned the Department's or my name at the date of the tribunal and I therefore took the precaution of asking the judge for his permission to have the case heard in camera. My name would in any case have been published but in view of the Blackpool Gazette's outcry I hoped to avoid any adverse effects upon the working of the Department. This was the sole reason for which I took the step and the tribunal agreed that the position of the Department should be safeguarded from prejudice. Subsequently, however, I understand that Mr. Robinson gave an interview to a daily paper and released the information for publication. In the meantime the Editor of the Blackpool Gazette published an editorial protesting against the secrecy which a judge had exercised his discretion to allow. In view of the tribunal's decision in my case it is difficult to understand Mr. Robinson's speeches on the matter as reported in the press, and it appears that any embarrassment which may have been caused to the Department has arisen entirely from the unsubstantiated statements he has made.

My activities are most clearly defined in the attached copy letters. My statement before the tribunal to the effects that I had become joint secretary of the Blackpool group was correct although I informed the tribunal at the time when the case was heard that I had ceased to hold the position after a period of some six weeks.

With regard to the proceedings before the tribunal I should perhaps mention I am advised that, in view of the order for the case to be heard in camera, my release of copies of the evidence and findings may amount to contempt of court.

Although it did not become necessary to elaborate upon the position during my evidence, Mr Baxter's letter defines what little work was entailed, comprising some very small amount of correspondence within a limited sphere. The discussion to which I referred concerned an average of less than half a dozen friends and dealt with the simple elements of general philosophy. The meetings of march 13th and April 10th were not public meetings and I have consistently refused to take part in such events.

Notwithstanding the overdrawn and undignified assertions of Mr. Robinson I cannot consider that my activities in Blackpool could be regarded as prejudicial to my position in the Department or contravening a fair interpretation of the principles of Establishment Leaflet No. 2. It seems from a statement made by the Editor of the Blackpool Gazette that there was a movement afoot to "wipe out" the P.P.U. in Blackpool. Information was obtained by some means and when close investigation disclosed my connection, the greatest advantage was taken of my being a civil servant.

In view of the events which I have occurred I do, however, appreciate that an interpretation of Establishment Leaflet No. 2 to a [degree of strictness] hitherto unrealised degree of strictness should be observed and perhaps the Board will take into account an assurance that in future my actions will be regulated to conform to this standard.

Signed W F Manthorpe

17th May 1940

Appendix 7

Poem written by Walter and sent to Mary.

On Reaching a Safe Area from London, 1940.

In each of the two hundred mundane miles
Subconscious incantations successively roll back
Scales of Crystallised reaction and my mind,
Disengaging from the vast gear of perpetual awareness
In the omnipresent fear,
Sags to laboured inactivity.

But beneath the artificial stimulation of normality
Senses resume an ordered activity and one
Becomes aware of an atmosphere, strange, but cast in a form,
Elusively pre-knowledged.

Can this be how life was before?

Is it possible that in these two hundred miles
Lies the difference between
Knowing and not knowing
Living and not living
Living and enduring?
We have lost the measured dull note that predicts the sudden
Clattering, shattering, whistling, screaming
In death-redolent night.
We are no longer the faithful, fearful puppets of a deity
Whose voice prompts absolute obedience through sickening discord
And marks the dusk and dawn with heavy emphasis.
We are not to be the passive subjects of exhumation
From a rubble-heap, once number ninety-two?

These roofs remain unruffled.
Colonnades of glass still give protection
From a wind which bears only Nature's onslaught
The air-raid warden remarks, 'We shall get it yet".
But clearly does not believe.
In the smoke haze of the café the tinkle of grandes dames
Vies with the chatter of tea cups.
They have not known the whine and clatter of shrapnel
From the smoke-burst in the sky.

They have not been subjected to the terror of the bed
From which security has fled.

Perhaps it is better so.

Bibliography

Aldington, Richard. *Life for Life's Sake.* London: Cassell, 1941.
Auden, W.H. *The Ascent of F6.* London: Faber & Faber, 1937.
Barrett, Clive *Subversive Peacemakers: War Resistance 1914-1918.* Cambridge: The Lutterworth Press, 2014.
Bibbings, Lois S. *Telling Tales About Men.* Manchester: Manchester University Press, 2009.
Blishen, Edward. *A Cack-Handed War.* London: Thanes & Hudson, 1972.
Blunden, Edmund. *Undertones of War.* London: Penguin, 1928.
Boulton, David. *Objection Overruled.* Letchworth: McGibbon & Key Ltd., 1967.
Brittain, Vera. *Testament of a Peace Lover.* London: Little Brown Book Group, 1988.
Brock, Peter. *Pacifism in Europe to 1914.* Princeton: Princeton University Press, 1972.
Brockway, Fenner. *Inside the Left.* London: George Allen & Unwin, 1942.
Browning, Stephen. *Norwich In the Great War.* Barnsley: Pen and Sword Military, 2015.
Burnham, Karyn. *The Courage of Cowards.* Barnsley: Pen and Sword History, 2014.
Ceadal, Michael. *Pacifism in Britain 1914-1945.* Oxford: Clarendon Press, 1980.
Chisholm, Anne. *Rumer Godden.* (revised and updated) London: Pan, 1999.
Clark, Christopher. *The Sleepwalkers. How Europe Went to War in 1914.* London: The Penguin Press, 2012.
Conyers, Bernard. *Never Forever.* London: Regency Press, 1958.
Debbage, Sue and Arrowsmith, Deb.
Gildencroft: Let Their Lives Speak. Norwich: Moofix, 2012.
Dowling, Timothy C. (Ed.)
Personal Perspectives: World War I. Santa Barbara, California: ABC Clio, 2006.
Du Cane, Sir Edmund F. *The Punishment and Prevention of Crime.* London: Macmillan & Co, 1885.

Eirug, Aled.	'Opposition to the First World War in Wales'. Thesis Submitted for the Degree of Doctor of Philosophy, Cardiff University, 2016.
Ferguson, Niall.	*The Pity of War 1914-1918.* London: The Penguin Press, 1998.
Geoghegan, Vincent.	*Socialism and Religion: Roads to Common Wealth.* London and New York: Routledge, 2011.
Godden, Rumer.	*A House With Four Rooms.* London: Corgi edition, 1999. [Originally Macmillan].
Goodall, Felicity.	*We Will Not Go To War: : Conscientious Objection During The World Wars.* Stroud. The History Press, 2010. [First published as *A Question of Conscience*, 1997.]
Graham, John, William.	*Conscription and Conscience, A History, 1916-1919.* London: George, Allen & Unwin, 1922.
Gregory, Adrian.	*The Last Great War. British Society and the First World War.* Cambridge: CUP, 2008.
Griffiths, Richard.	*What Did You Do During the War.* Oxford: Routledge, 2017.
Hayes, Dennis.	*Challenge of Conscience.* London: George Allen & Unwin, 1949.
Holland, James.	*The War in the West.* London: Transworld, 2015.
Huxley, Aldous.	*Ends and Means.* Edinburgh: Readers' Union & Chatto and Windus, 1938.
Hynes, Samuel.	*A War Imagined: The First World War and English Culture.* London: Bodley Head, 1990.
Kramer, Ann.	*Conscientious Objectors of the First World War: A Determined Resistance.* Barnsley: Pen and Sword Social History, 2014.
Kramer, Ann.	*Conscientious Objectors of the Second World War: Refusing to Fight.* Barnsley: Pen and Sword Social History, 2013.
Meeres, Frank.	*Dorothy Jewson: Suffragette and Socialist.* Cromer: Poppyland Publishing, 2014.
Milne, A.A.	*Peace with Honour.* New York: E.P. Dutton & Co Ltd. 1935 (Revised edition)
Moorehead, Caroline.	*Troublesome People: The Warriors of Pacifism.* London: Hamish Hamilton, 1986.
Mottram, R.H.	*The Spanish Farm.* London: Chatto & Windus, 1924.

Mottram, R.H.	*The Window Seat or Life Observed.* London: Hutchinson & Co., 1954.
Mowat, Charles Loch.	*Britain Between the Wars 1918-1940.* London: Methuen & Co, 1955.
Oakley, Ann.	*Man and wife: Richard and Kay Titmuss: My parents' early years.* London: Flamingo, 1997.
Overy, Richard.	*The Morbid Age: Britain Between the Wars.* London: Allen Lane, 2009.
Palmer, Alan.	*Victory 1918.* New York: Atlantic Monthly Press, 1998.
Rae, John.	*Conscience & Politics.* London: Oxford University Press, 1970.
Rank, Carol (Ed.).	*City of Peace: Bradford's Story.* Bradford: Bradford Libraries, 1997.
Raymond, Ernest.	*Tell England.* London: Cassell, 1922.
Smith, Angela K.	*The Second Battlefield. Women, Modernism and the First World War.* Manchester: Manchester University Press, 2000.
Smith, Helen Zenna.	*Not So Quiet....* New York: The Feminist Press, 1989. [First Published London, Albert E, Marriot, 1930].
Spencer, Colin.	*The Heretic's Feast: A History of Vegetarianism.* Hanover and London: University Press of New England, 1995. [Originally published by Fourth Estate 1993].
Stuart, Tristram.	*The Bloodless Revolution: A Cultural History of Vegetarianism from 1600 to Modern Times.* New York: W.W. Norton & Company, 2007. [First published by Harper Press 2006.]
Swinnerton, Frank.	*The Georgian Literary Scene.* London: Hutchinson & Co, 1935.
Thwaite, Ann.	*A.A. Milne: The Man Behind Winnie-the-Pooh.* London: Random House, 1990.
Triston, H.U.	*Men in Cages.* Book Club, 1938.
Wade, Francesca.	*Square Haunting.* London, Faber 2020.
Wallis, Jill.	*Valiant for Peace: A History of the Fellowship of Reconciliation 1914-1989.* London: Fellowship of Reconciliation, 1991.
Wiltsher, Anne.	*Most Dangerous Women: Feminist Peace Campaigners of the Great War.* London: Pandora Press, 1985.

Articles

Eastern Daily Press, 3 January 1979, p. 6, Jonathan Mardle, 'An Advocate of Health'.

Eastern Daily Press, 29 December 1979, Obituary, 'Founder of city health store dies'.

History Today, Volume 68 Issue 11, November 2018, Alice Brumby, 'When the Men Came Marching Home'.

Websites

https://www.leeds.ac.uk/news/article/3695/legacies_of_war_conscientious_objectors_records_in_digital_memorial, accessed 13/04/2021.

https://peaceandjustice.org.uk/what-we-do/legacies-of-resistance-to-first-world-war-in-scotland/, accessed 13/04/2021.

https://en.wikipedia.org/wiki/Third_Zimmerwald_Conference, accessed 19/04/2021.

Hulonce, Lesley, https://ahrc.ukri.org/research/fundedthemesandprogrammes/worldwaroneanditslegacy/world-war-one-at-home/ww1inwales/pulpitsmutinieskhakifever/, accessed 21/09/21.

https://ahrc.ukri.org/research/fundedthemesandprogrammes/worldwaroneanditslegacy/world-war-one-at-home/ww1inwales/pulpitsmutinieskhakifever/, accessed 28/08/21.

https://dartmoorcollective.org/featured-content/the-conscientious-objectors-road/

Index

Allen, C. 36, 191
Archer, T. 71, 89
Arnold
  Algernon F. 108
  Harry 108, 111, 112, 173
  Mrs. 112
Arnold, Hans 132
Arnold Son & Hedley 108, 117
Ashley family
  Austin 71
  Donald 62
  Jack 42, 68, 71, 77, 82, 90, 91, 96, 101
  Lewis 68
  Richard 51, 55, 59
Asquith, Viscount 17
Auden, W.H. 14, 113, 128, 173
Ballachulish, Scotland 57, 63
Banfield
  Bernard 118, 126, 176
  Elsie 127
Baxter, R. 42, 148, 185
Blackpool Peace Pledge Union 145, 147
Bloomsbury Group, The 35, 129
Bloomsbury House 127
Blyth, Dr. 42
Boddy, P.J. 28, 38, 76
Brace, W. 39
Brockway
  Fenner, MP 15, 36, 49, 105, 153
  Jack 110, 111
Cadbury, J.J. 26
Caolasnacon, Scotland 62, 64, 65, 68
Catchpole, J.E. 158
Cavell, Edith 27, 101, 174
Ceadel, M. 13, 16, 45, 46, 48
Central Board of Conscientious Objectors 141, 153

Chadwick, W. 170
Christian Pacifist Forestry and Land Unit 153
Christian, P.C. 170
Citizens of Tomorrow, Guild of 117
Copeman
  Mrs. 26
  Thomas 31
Crane, Geoffrey 110, 117, 135
Dartmoor 56, 57, 60–62, 71, 79, 80–85, 86, 87, 92, 95, 96, 97
Davison, W., Sir 143
Day, H. 7, 22, 25, 35, 78, 79, 112, 139
Defence of the Realm Act 101
Derby, Earl of 18, 40
Dixon, J.H. 122, 173
Duncan, H. 45
Eddington family 26
  Alexander (A.E.) 1847-1929 26, 36, 38
  Arthur John (A.J.) 1886-1946 28, 142
  Florence, 2nd wife of Alexander 42, 76, 91
  shop (Gentleman's Walk) 27, 174
Einstein, Albert 105, 106
Evans, A. 72, 175
Exposition Internationale 113
Federation of British Youth Movements 120
Fellowship of Reconciliation 40, 105
Firth, W.H. 87–88, 90, 91, 94
  death & funeral 93
Gandhi, Mahatma 106
Goat Lane Meeting 7, 23, 24
Gregory, J. 128, 132, 154
Hammond, E. 178
Hardie, K. 35
Home Office Scheme 39, 46, 54, 56, 57, 58, 61, 63, 68, 72, 76, 77, 87
Huxley, A. 115, 144
International Women's Congress 105
Isherwood, C. 113, 128
Jackman, F. 12, 118, 176

Jermy
　A. 38
　Matilda, née Manthorpe 7, 8, 20, 24, 26, 29, 36, 37, 46
Joad, C.M. 15, 132, 153
Kimberley, Lord 41
Kinloch-Cooke, C., Sir 62
Kitchener, Lord 17, 18, 41
Krishnamurti, J. 121, 129
Lansbury, G. 105, 123, 143, 183
League of Nations Union 105, 107, 108
Leslie, Osmond 128, 133, 144, 178
Lloyd George, David 41, 47
Lloyd, R.O. 170
Macauley, R. 15, 153
Macdonald, Ramsay 66
Maddermarket Theatre 109, 128
Manthorpe family 20
　Andrew 20
　Annie (Anne) 20
　Eliza, née Land 20, 21, 29
　George 20, 21
　Hamilton 7, 20, 21, 23, 24, 25, 26, 29, 112, 168, 170, 192
　Jack 101, 142
　Matilda. *See* Jermy: Matilda, née Manthorpe
　Walter 13, 20, 28, 31, 42, 45, 49, 56, 57, 122, 173, 178
　Walter Frederick 143, 145, 148
Marshall, C. 36
Marsh, H. 161, 166, 167
McFadden, B. 30
Menon, V.K. Krishna 121
Military Service Act 18, 40, 45
Milne, A.A. 15, 153
Monck, N. 109
Mottram, R.H. 104
National Association of Health stores 104, 111
Newby, W. 76, 86, 87

No-Conscription Fellowship (NCF) 38, 87, 97, 104
No More War Movement 14, 104, 117, 143
Pankhurst
　Celia 177
　Sylvia 66
Parker, A. 15, 122, 124, 135, 178
Peace Army 106
Peace Pledge Union 9, 38, 56, 57, 87, 105, 115, 123, 125, 128, 132, 133, 139, 143, 144, 145, 147, 149, 150, 153, 184, 185
Pelham Committee 39, 78
Pitman's Vegetarian Hotel 72, 77
Price, Philip 135
Princeton workcamp 8, 59, 61, 62, 63, 83, 85, 90, 92, 97, 191
Read, A. 75
Reilly family
　Gerard (Nunc) 118, 119, 175
　Michael (Reilly) 175
　Myra née Jones 175
Roberts, E.G. 75, 86
Robinson, J.R., MP 148, 149, 150, 151
Russell, Bertrand 15, 35, 66, 78, 132, 153
Seago, E. 128
Shepherd, R. (Dick) 154, 177
Shields, W. 119, 133, 154, 155
Society of Friends (Quakers) 7, 21, 24, 27, 35, 36, 39, 40, 43, 58, 72, 92, 118, 127, 148, 184, 187
　Quakerism (beliefs) 15
Soper, D. 105
Stockholm Conference 70, 71, 75
Swann family
　Frederick William 88, 111
　Jane 31, 32
Swingler, R. 128, 133, 154, 155
Talgarth, Wales 58, 70, 73, 77, 88, 96
The Ascent of F6 113, 128
Theatre Royal, Norwich 111
Theosophical Society 117
　Theosophy (beliefs) 15

Titmuss, R. 15, 118, 120, 129

Tolstoy 106, 127, 131

Tolstoy (play) 127

Val Baker, D. 154, 178

Wakefield Prison 58, 69, 70

War Resisters' International 105

War Resisters' Triennial Conference, Lyon 106

Women's International League of Peace and Freedom 105

Wootton, B. 138

World Anti-War Congress, Amsterdam 106

World Disarmament Conference 106

Wormwood Scrubs 46, 49, 50, 52, 53, 54, 55, 56, 61, 75, 86, 87

Youth House 13, 15, 117–123, 125, 127, 128, 131, 132, 133, 136, 138, 139, 141, 144, 150, 151, 154, 155, 173, 175

Printed in Great Britain
by Amazon